WORSHIP ANTHOLOGY

WORSHIP ANTHOLOGY

A Collection of Worship Resources by
Women Ordained to Word & Sacrament

Edited by

SHEILA CRAGGS, ELEANOR MACALISTER,
ALISON MEHIGAN and PAULINE STEENBERGEN

SAINT ANDREW PRESS
EDINBURGH

First published in 2008 by
SAINT ANDREW PRESS
121 George Street, Edinburgh EH2 4YN

Copyright © The Contributors 2008

ISBN 978 0 7152 0851 9

References in the text to Bible versions are as follows:

AV	=	Authorised Version
GNB	=	Good News Bible
Msg	=	The Message
NEB	=	New English Bible
NIV	=	New International Version
NRSV	=	New Revised Standard Version
REB	=	Revised English Bible
RSV	=	Revised Standard Version

British Library Cataloguing in Publication Data
A catalogue record for this book is available from the British Library

It is the publisher's policy to only use papers that are natural and recyclable and that have been manufactured from timber grown in renewable, properly managed forests. All of the manufacturing processes of the papers are expected to conform to the environmental regulations of the country of origin.

Typeset in Palatino and Frutiger by Waverley Typesetters, Fakenham
Printed and bound by Bell & Bain Limited, Glasgow

Contents

Part One
PRACTICAL RESOURCES

Contents

Part Two
THE INSPIRATION BEHIND THE
WORSHIP ANTHOLOGY

Part One
PRACTICAL RESOURCES

Section 1
Sacraments

A Silent Communion

REV. MARGARET STEIN

I was involved as the art tutor in a Painting and Prayer Retreat at Llanghasty, an Anglican Retreat House in Wales a few years before women were ordained in the Church of England. The chaplain was keen that I should celebrate the Lord's Supper one morning, and told the group. I then spent a day convincing the nuns who ran the place and the group members that this was in order. Realising that there were so many problems for people, I decided (1) that, since we kept silence overnight, to celebrate the sacrament in silence might at least get over the problem of people hearing unfamiliar words in a female voice; and (2) to include a time of prayer for each other.

Silent Communion

I worked out a series of mime-movements to suggest the different parts of the service following the Anglican Service Book, and made sure each participant had a copy of the Bible and a note of the reading for that day. There was a beautiful carved image of Jesus as King at the front of the chapel, so I could use that as a reference point. Afterwards, I realised that it would have been helpful to use a little bell to indicate when different parts of the service started. Others have devised silent Communion services, but I was not aware of this at the time.

Praying for each other

I used a way of praying for each other which I had learned from Canon Shells, one of the founders of the then Painting and Prayer Retreat Movement. We were seated in a circle. As the worship leader at the time, I started by standing and going to the person on my left, gently laying hands on her head and praying in silence for her for a short time. Then I moved on to the second and then the third person. At that point, the first person I had prayed for stood up and went to pray similarly for the second person. When I moved on to the fourth, the first person after me could move to the third, and when I moved to the fifth, the first could move to the fourth, and the second person could then go to pray for the third. And so we followed one another round until I sat down and then was prayed for by each of the others in turn. Eventually, each of us had prayed for the other, and been prayed for, and were back in our own seats. This takes a long time, so is not recommended if there are more than about a dozen present; but, by the end, the presence of the Lord is almost tangible.

These actions worked well, as they resolved the difficulty of this particular situation where there was concern about having a woman as celebrant. However, they also fitted into the retreat situation where people were in silence. And praying for each other in this way led to a strong sense of the presence of God and His love holding the group and situation, and meant that we could share in the sacrament together.

A Communion Liturgy

REV. JANE DENNISTON

I wanted to write something which had elements of the tradition but expressed something of what I felt; something that was creatively liturgical, with poetic but accessible language. This liturgy can be easily adapted for small or large groups and lends itself to a variety of situations.

1 CALL TO WORSHIP

Leader:	In this familiar feast
ALL:	**Jesus meets us**
Leader:	To banish our darkness with his light
ALL:	**God with us**
Leader:	In ancient patterns made new
ALL:	**His Spirit is here**
Leader:	Let us worship God.

2 ACTION *Reader 1*

The Light shone in the darkness, and the darkness has not put it out. (*Light a candle.*)

3 PRAISE

4 OPENING PRAYER

Lord, if we did not praise you,
    if our mouths were to fall silent,

the very stones would cry out in praise of your
wonderful deeds.
Lord, if we did not praise you,
if our eyes were blind to your glory,
the very heavens would declare your greatness
and majesty.
Lord, if we did not praise you,
if our hearts were cold to your love,
all creation would bow before you and worship
your glorious name.
But we will worship you.
And in this time of worship, we join with all creation
in declaring
that you alone are worthy of our praise.
Conscious of your glory, Lord,
we are also conscious of our sin.
In our thoughts we forsake you.
(*Silence*)
In our words we dishonour you.
(*Silence*)
In our deeds we offend you.
(*Silence*)
In what we leave undone we abandon you.
(*Silence*)

Forgive our sin, Lord,
and lead us in new ways, of hope, of compassion and of
grace.
Lord, have mercy
Christ, have mercy
Lord, have mercy.

We thank you for that mercy which is always more ready
to forgive
than we are to admit our fault,

and we open our lives
    to your life-giving breath,
    to your cleansing rain,
    to your refining fire,
that we may live more truly as your people
in the name of Christ our Saviour, Amen.

5   READING

6   REFLECTION

7   THE INVITATION

This is the table of our Lord
where hurts are healed,
failures restored
and all is made new in the love of God.
Come, bring nothing but your love
because your Lord invites you.
Taste and see that the Lord is good.

8   THE STORY *Reader 2*

Let's hear the story of how this began.
On the night on which Jesus was betrayed, he sat at
    supper with his disciples.
While they were eating, he took a piece of bread, said a
    blessing, broke it and gave it to them with the words:
'This is my body. It is broken for you. Do this to remember
    me.'
Later, he took a cup of wine, saying:
'This cup is God's new covenant, sealed with
    my blood. Drink from it, all of you, to remember me.'

So now, we do as Jesus did, and as he said; we take this
   bread and this wine,
ordinary things and temporal which he makes unique and
   eternal,
and through these we will have communion with one
another and with him.

9 EUCHARISTIC PRAYER (THANKSGIVING)

Let us pray.

Leader: For friends and fellowship,
            for freedom and time to worship,
            for gifts of love and grace
            We praise you.
ALL: THANK YOU, GOD.

Leader: You made all things.
            and without you we cannot even draw
               breath.
            For this we praise you.
ALL: THANK YOU, GOD.

Leader: We praise you for the grace which allows
               us to come into your presence.
            We praise you for the faithfulness which
               waits for us when we turn from you.
            We praise you for the love which
               welcomes us with open arms.
            For all this we praise you.
ALL: THANK YOU, GOD.

            And here at this table as we offer
               the fruit of our hands
               and a sacrifice of praise,

you offer your very self,
> the sacrifice of your broken body
> and your shed blood
so that we may be forgiven,
> healed, filled, blessed
>> and made new again.
And in gratitude we join our voices to
> those of the Church on earth and in
> heaven:

ALL: **HOLY, HOLY, HOLY LORD,**
GOD OF POWER AND MIGHT,
HEAVEN AND EARTH ARE FULL OF
> **YOUR GLORY,**
HOSANNA IN THE HIGHEST,

BLESSED IS HE WHO COMES
IN THE NAME OF THE LORD.
HOSANNA IN THE HIGHEST.

10 PRAYER OF CONSECRATION

Lord, we praise you and thank you
> for your creativity in the world,
>> and your covenant with us.
We thank you, generous Jesus,
> that as a baby you came into this world;
>> that you lived and laughed.
That in all humanity
> you surprised and shocked,
>> worked and wept,
>>> suffered and sacrificed.
We thank you, startling Jesus,
> that for us you rose from death
>> and ascended to heaven.

That in your grace and mercy
>   you poured out your Holy Spirit upon us
>   and pray for us always,
>   and that you will come again in glory and
>   power.

So now as we remember and recreate what you did in an
>   upstairs room,
we ask you to send down your Holy Spirit on us
and on these gifts of bread and wine
>   that they may become for us your body;
>   health,
>   wholeness
>   and holiness
to the glory of God,
Father, Son and Holy Spirit.

Let us say together the prayer that Jesus taught us:

11 LORD'S PRAYER

Our Father ...

12 BREAKING OF BREAD

(*Taking and breaking the bread*)
Around a table, among friends, Jesus took bread.
As he broke it, he said:
'This is my body, it is broken for you.'

(*Taking the cup of wine*)
And later, he took the cup of wine and said:
'This is the new relationship with God,
your birth through my death.
Take this, all of you, to remember me.

This is your Lord, in bread and in wine
For you.
Take and eat.'
(*Communion is shared*)

13   THE PEACE

The peace of the Father of joy
The peace of the Christ of hope
The peace of the Spirit of grace
Let's share it now.
The Lord's peace be with you all.

14   CONCLUDING PRAYER

Leader: Here we have tasted the things of this world.
Here we have touched the things of the next.
Here we have seen and heard of the great
    mystery of our salvation.
Here we have eaten of one loaf,
    and drunk of one cup,
    in that communion becoming one
        with you,
        with our brothers and sisters
        near and far
    and with that great cloud of witnesses
    which surrounds us.
May this precious gift which we have
    received
    be shared with all whose lives we
        touch,
    that our love of you
    and your love in us
    may shine for the salvation of the
        world.
Amen.
ALL: **AMEN.**

15 ACTION

Pass round a basket of white ribbons as a symbol of our cleansing. Each takes one and ties it round his/her neighbour's wrist as a symbol of our dependence on one another.

Or: anoint one another with oil in the sign of the cross.

16 PRAISE

17 CLOSING

ALL: **For darkness you give light**
For despair you give hope
For confusion you give peace
For sorrow you give joy
For ourselves you give yourself.
Let us go
In peace, in love, in joy
And in the company of our Saviour.
Amen.

The Ironing-Board Communion

REV. ELEANOR MACALISTER

'Climb every mountain' was the title of my final address to the congregation of Ellon Parish Church on 29 October 2006. Both worship and Communion were celebrated from an ironing board – and remarkably this ordinary household task took on something of a priestly significance. It is the story of one woman's journey in ministry. I am fond of cooking – and so, in the manner of a cookery book, it's essential to gather together your ingredients and follow the instructions. So ... read on.

READINGS: Ephesians 5:6–10 and Mark 8:31–8

Ingredients

One ironing board, one iron, one extension cable, two linen baskets, one filled with laundry needing ironed. The other holds a Communion cup filled with wine and a Communion plate holding a loaf, both items covered by a white tablecloth. From a distance, this just looks like another basket of laundry.

Method

Have the ironing board, iron and two linen baskets set up centrally on the chancel area prior to worship beginning. Ensure iron is plugged in. The linen baskets should be within easy reach. Conduct worship from the ironing board. When it is time for the address, 'Climb Every Mountain', switch on iron, and iron the laundry from time to time as one is talking. Cease ironing each time an extract is read.

'Climb Every Mountain'

Seeing me standing here ironing this morning is probably causing some of you to say to yourselves: 'Eleanor has finally cracked!' But, in fairness to myself, I think that many of you know that it's been pretty hectic in the manse recently. We've been gutting for what seems like months. There's a pile of stuff in the garage as high as my Mini ... all of it going to good homes, except my car of course ... and the ironing has been piling up. So I thought I'd bring it in here this morning, as Gary is running out of shirts.

I love ironing! It's the one household job I sincerely enjoy. Isn't it lovely when you iron laundry fresh off the washing-line? What a glorious smell.

It's therapeutic, ironing, as far as I'm concerned. I can switch off as I watch the creases disappear. I can stand and mull things over in my mind. In fact, I have a notepad at the side of the ironing board because often, in this relaxed state of being, I have ideas for a sermon or an All-Age Worship idea or a prayer coming to mind. That's when God sees an inroad into my often scrambled mind ... taps me on the shoulder ... and has a word with me.

It was when I was ironing one day that I felt God calling me to the ministry. It was a bit of a shock, I can tell you. Not the sort of thing you'd expect while standing at an ironing board. I recall finishing the ironing and putting it away with this amazing feeling in my tummy. It was great! And, just to make sure I wasn't imagining it, I got the clothes I'd just ironed, crumpled them up a bit ... and yes, you've guessed it ... began to iron them again. And the feeling ... the sense of Call ... was there ... as strong as it had been ten minutes before. Ironing took on a different dimension! For many weeks, our children were the smartest-dressed in the school! And I had a very smug look on my face!

Voice 1

Wednesday 14 December 1988.

This week, I had an experience that I have found both exciting and depressing. I have experienced the call to be a minister in the Church of Scotland.

> *Exciting – because I have finally admitted to myself that this is what I want to do.*

> *Depressing – because I feel there is so much against me being able to fulfil this need.*

This call has been niggling and worrying away at me for what seems years. It is something I have fought against time after time, almost to the point of denying Christ.

I put up many barriers, but they came down when I eventually admitted to Gary two weeks ago that this is what I wanted to do. It was through my own admission to him that I finally admitted it to myself and to God.

I feel a great sense of relief and yet a great turmoil. I can't think straight and have sometimes lost track of the days of the week. How can I be a worthy wife and mother and minister? That is what I find so depressing. I can't deny my family – but I can't deny this calling. I have been unable to sleep properly. The symptoms are similar to finding out that one is in love! Perhaps I will look back with cynicism on what I have written here – but I doubt it!

So the process began. Application to the Church of Scotland Board of Ministry. The dreaded Selection School process! The acceptance, second time round, and four wonderful years at Aberdeen University. These were exciting times … and I managed to continue to be a mum and a wife and a student and gain a Second Class

Honours (Division One). Talk about multi-tasking! And God was there every step of the way.

A high point in this whole initial process was the Licensing Service. This was a special moment, organised by the Church Presbytery. In those days, that was the moment when you became a Rev. and could wear a dog collar!

Voice 2

27 June 1993

Lord, this evening has to be the best! I will treasure every word spoken at my Licensing Service, and I can only say 'thank you' for all you have done through so many people. Thanks also for the amount of pleasure this occasion has brought to family and friends.

From responding to the call way back in 1988, there have been many highs and not many lows. In 1997, for example, I achieved something I had always dreamed of ever since I was a wee girl – to go on a pilgrimage to the Holy Land, which I led.

Voice 3

Day 2. Wednesday 5 February 1997. (My 45th birthday!)

Early rise – 6:30a.m. Set off for Jerusalem at 8:10a.m.

Netanya to Jerusalem – gave us all a wonderful opportunity to see the countryside.

Jerusalem – our first stop was the Mount of Olives – from the top we viewed the panorama of the Dome of the Rock, the El Acqsa Mosque, the Zion Gate and Golden Gate. We began with a prayer. From the top of the Mount of Olives, you can see the original 'city' of Jerusalem – a Jebusite settlement – tiny! Church of St Peter of Gallicantu – the cock crowed three times. Down in the dungeons and at the bottom level of the excavations, read Peter's denial from the Good News Bible. Very moving. Evening at hotel – very jolly! Phoned home. What a birthday!

The journey – my journey – so far has been quite amazing. I liken it to climbing mountains. I guess, like anyone who is into rock-climbing or even mountain-climbing, the trick is to try to keep looking upwards, looking out for finger-holds, looking downwards and sideways from time to time to ensure that your feet are firmly in the grooves or foot-holds.

Like climbers, there have been times when I have felt my fingers slipping, scrabbling for some firm hold, digging in hard when in danger of falling. At the time of my breast-cancer experience, I felt that I was clinging to a steep cliff by my fingernails. Like climbers, it's been essential to check the equipment … and, like a lot of climbers, I have climbed not on my own, but with those with a similar passion and a deep-seated faith in God.

When I've reached the top of a peak, the view has generally been marvellous. Maybe it has been clouded over at times, but there is always an amazing panorama with lots more mountains to climb in the distance! Lots more challenges!

Just last week, when I was talking to a friend about what I was planning to do this morning, something occurred to me – and it's this. When you stand at the top of a mountain range, you often see the shadows of the clouds scudding across the landscape. This creates varying shades of green below the tree-line. And, where the sun's rays don't reach the slopes and valleys at certain times of the day, there are shadows.

How like life.

For sometimes we are steeped in the bright sunshine that is joy … and yet … sometimes joy is as fickle as wind-driven clouds. Sometimes it seems that we are living in shadows where the sun doesn't seem to shine.

How like life.

How like the Good Shepherd of whom we sing so often, walking with us in the peaks and troughs of life. And yes, through the valley of the shadow of death.

How like those two old familiar 23rd Psalmers, like old friends and companions who, if we look over our shoulder, we will see walking behind us or climbing alongside us … 'goodness' and 'love' … who will be with us all our lives.

For God has promised this.
Shadows.

How like your life, and how like mine.

In my mind's eye, as I look across to the next mountain, there is an outstanding hill which seems to get in the way. There is a cross on it, throwing its own shadow. That shadow of the cross, for me, is inescapable. That was when, in chatting to my friend, I fully realised that my ministry has been carried out in the shadow of the cross. That makes me glad and brings me a deep sense of comfort. As night turns into day and day turns into night, that shadow was, and still is, there; as I sat at a hospital bed or chatting in a shop; or wiping up the sick of a young lad who'd had too much to drink and was afraid to go home; or alone in my car; or as the life and soul of the party … the shadow was always there reminding me of whom I serve … unconditionally.

And that call to follow, to serve, is as much for you as it is for me.

It's a call that takes you to the heights and drops you to the depths.

It's a call to walk in a path of radical love that challenges, for example, power structures.

It's a call that can lead to danger because we live out this call in the midst of overwhelming forces that try to remove our focus on what is most important.

In Mark's Gospel, there is a powerful sense that mountains need to be climbed by Jesus, with the journey leading ever closer to Jerusalem, that hill and that cross. But Mark never suggests that suffering and death are *God's* will for Jesus … or for his disciples …

or for you ... or for me. I do not believe that God brings suffering upon people.

I believe that we need to get our heads round the fact that Jesus did not desire execution. We need only to revisit the words he prayed in the Garden of Gethsemane. Nor did he see sacrifice as a virtue either. What he did do was his Father's will – and he accepted, apparently with fear and trembling, his death as the inevitable consequence of living an all-encompassing life of love ... a love that challenged oppressive power structures and all those things that get in the way of the relationship between people and God. I am more and more convinced that suffering is a consequence of discipleship ... I would push this even further to say that suffering is a consequence of sacrifice. I know, as many others know, that responding to the tap on the shoulder brings its own demands. Equally, though, I am also certain that God never asks us to do anything he believes we cannot do.

During a workshop I was attending a few years ago in St Andrews for the DMin (that, as you know, I didn't quite complete!), I was suddenly overwhelmed by the immensity of the task into which I was entering. Gary phoned on the first evening to hear his wife stating that she couldn't do it ... it was too much ... she was going to give up there and then. She was coming home. His response? 'Eleanor. How do you eat an elephant?' My response? 'I don't do elephants! How do you eat an elephant?' To which he replied: 'In little chunks!'

So, for all of us here this morning, I ask:

- those who have climbed mountains on your own and with me;
- those who have more to climb;
- those who feel that they're facing the insurmountable task of eating an elephant:

What are the possible consequences of your call to serve?
What do you most fear?

And, amid all your fears and questions, what I would suggest is this: remember that Mark's Jesus did not call people to walk the path of discipleship alone, but rather to do so in loving community. One of the greatest joys for me has been to be part of the loving and hospitable community that is Ellon Parish Church, for

- together, we've ironed out lots of creases!
- we've discovered so many hidden treasures as we've raked about in the laundry basket of life!
- we've had gutting sessions and made numerous visits to the recycling bins!
- we have a community that strives to live out its calling in the shadow of the cross.

And so it has to be that my prayer for this community that I love dearly is this: build upon all of this with your new minister; work together; climb together; enjoy the views from the top; celebrate; tackle each task a wee bit at a time, and know that to follow Jesus Christ means not only to walk in his path up the mountains and down in the valleys, but also to be in a loving, non-judgemental and intimate relationship with him ... and with the God who taps people like you and like me on the shoulder in the most interesting and surprising of ways! Live like people who belong to the light, and try to learn what pleases the Lord. For it is to him that we give all glory and praise.   AMEN.

By the end of the address, I had completed ironing the laundry in the first basket. After I said 'Amen, and may God bless to us this preaching of his Holy Word', I reached into the second basket, took out the white linen cloth which, incidentally, had a hole in it, placed it on the ironing board and began to iron it carefully. It covered the ironing board nicely. I then took out the Communion plate with the bread and placed it carefully on the ironing board. I took out the Communion cup filled with wine and placed it carefully on the ironing board too. All this was done in complete silence.

The table was set.
The Invitation was extended.
The bread and wine were set apart.
An ordinary ironing board was set apart.
We celebrated the Sacrament of the Lord's Supper
around an extraordinary ironing board.

Communion Circle Prayer

REV. RACHEL DOBIE

The prayer, a circle prayer, expresses something of the nature of God. The sharing with my probationer in the sacrament of Holy Communion mirrored the sense of companionship that had been the hallmark of my probationer's time with me and the congregation.

I offer this suggestion for Holy Communion, which was used at the united farewell service for Frances Henderson, who had spent her probationary period in the four parishes of which I am minister.

It was a service for all ages, and there were many children present. I had not expected more than fifty to attend, since it was New Year's Day; but we actually had about eighty, and it was too late to change any plans we had made.

We wanted the worship to be dignified but relaxed, and so there were no white cloths except for veiling the elements; no great entry, and the elders were part of the body of the congregation, not seated round the table. A short order of Holy Communion from *Worship Now* was used.

Frances shared in the liturgy. The congregation was invited to leave the pews and stand in a group round the Communion table (which is on a slightly raised chancel area) between the Institution and the Prayer of Thanksgiving. This they did, old and young together, though not in the tidy rows as on a Galilee hillside.

When it came to the distribution, we took the now broken home-made loaf and passed the pieces round, collecting what was left.

Some of our congregations use a common cup and some glasses. When it came to the distribution of the wine, we each, Frances and I, lifted one cup and napkin and one tray of glasses, having explained before we started that they could receive from either of us.

There was something deeply moving to see hands reaching out for our very ancient cups made for the valley in which some of the communicants now lived and worked. After the prayer and the Peace, they returned to the pews.

When I had planned it, it did seem slightly risky. We were both so glad we had done it. We celebrated in the same way the following New Year.

Prayer of Approach and Confession

Lord, you are to us a circle;
in you there is no beginning, no end.
When you enfold us, you hold us, and so we praise you,
there is no place where you are not;
when the circle faces outwards
no one is hidden from your sight, no one excluded from your
presence,
and so we praise you.
Father, you are time itself,
and yet you are without time.
There was no time when you were not,
there can be no time when you will not be.
And for that sense of infinity, we praise you.
Yet there are times when we try to hide from you;
hide the fact that our lives are not
centred on you;
that we slip into the shadows cast by our own
and the world's selfishness and greed.
Forgive us, for we recognise our own imperfections.
Draw us out of the darkness,
Change us, cleanse us, restore us, we pray.

(*Silence*)
Know that God in his love and mercy forgives you and calls
you to his side.
AMEN.

The Guild and the Kitchen Table

REV. ALISON MEHIGAN

This meditation was used for an informal Communion at a Church of Scotland Guild dedication service, but it can be used and adapted to any informal Communion worship. A simple, old, bare kitchen table was used, and, after the meditation, the members of the Guild helped to set the table for Communion.

READING: Exodus 25:23–30 – The Table

As I stand at this table, we all realise it is not made of fancy acacia wood. The mouldings and trims are not of pure gold. In fact, the table itself is nothing special. Just wood, solid though, and with the odd scratch and dent that comes with the passage of time.

So often I have sat at my table at home, with a mug of coffee in one hand and a chocolate biscuit sitting sadly within too easy reach of the other. Nothing strange in that, you might think – an everyday occurrence in many homes.

In our homes, it is so often the kitchen table that is at the centre of all activity. When we have visitors, it doesn't seem to matter how clean and tidy we make the rest of the house; people will always congregate in the kitchen, no-one wants to miss out on what's going on there.

The table is more than a surface from which we eat meals, though it is that as well. It is a place where much conversation takes place, both during and following meals.

In younger days, it was a place where I sat when my knees were scraped from a fall, and my mum would clean me up and tend to me before I dashed out the door to do more damage.

It was a place of fun and play, anything from a ship to a tent, and certainly a fall-back hiding place if all other places failed and I was being sought!

In fact, in my schooldays, it was the place I studied for my exams, the other prime spots having been booked by my elder brothers and sister. In truth, I preferred the kitchen table, though I didn't let on to the others, for then I was always at hand when my mum was dishing out special treats.

The table was the place where my mum baked all the bread and, no doubt, unknown to us children, thumped out all her frustrations with routine daily life.

The table was a place where emotions could run high, and tea and sympathy were dished out in gallons. It was the place of comfort and compassion. It was where you discussed the latest fall-out with your best friend at school and where you discussed, in confidence, your first crush!

The table was all these things and more, for it was also the place that we as a family held hands, and said grace, and gave thanks for what God had provided.

And so, as we gather here this evening, I am ever mindful of how this humble table is symbolic of our Church, and of the Guild. Each, places where people gather, where there is a sense of community, a sense of belonging and sharing. Places where meals are served. Places where the Word is read and prayers are said and hands are held. Places where the heart can be opened and there will be no condemnation. Places where the community can be themselves and experience the sense of love and fellowship – and, in the stillness, sense God's presence.

Well, what then is our role? What are we expected to do when tending this symbolic table? Chief cook or bottle-washer? Yes, sometimes, but perhaps more importantly we are each called to serve.

Serve the table, clear the mess, listen to the conversations and offer whatever assistance is required. Of course, we can join in with the moments of laughter and tears too, but we are also there to enable and to encourage the growth of this family. And we must also make sure the family offers a sincere welcome to all who come.

This table may not be made of acacia wood. The cup and plate are not solid gold. But this humble table is central to this community – this community of people who have a sense of God's presence.

It is a place of fellowship, a place where people not only have a relationship with one another but also have a living and personal relationship with God.

The gathering therefore becomes a place where people are united and nurtured – and, more than that, a place where they are fed and rested and strengthened by God's presence.

And, as we sit round this table this evening, always keep in mind that everyone gathered here is basically just the same. Each of us on a journey with God, each of us led by the Spirit, and each of us inspired by the teaching and actions of Jesus.

A family of people on a journey of faith.

Welcome, welcome to this table.

After the table was set, a simple Communion liturgy was used, and the minister served each person personally.

A Baptismal Hymn

REV. LEZLEY KENNEDY

This hymn, set to a familiar tune, celebrates, in ordinary language, the significance of baptism and also the blessing of children. This is one woman minister's attempt to create a hymn that is meaningful and understandable for all!

'As the Church, the family of God' (sung to the tune – Sussex Carol)

> As the Church, the family of God,
> We gather round the font today.
> To welcome, pray for, and baptise,
> this child into the Christian Way.
> We come with joy to celebrate,
> the love that brings this little one.
>
> We come remembering Christ our Lord,
> Baptised himself God's chosen Son.
> And here responding to his life,
> by water's sign this child's made one,
> With God, through Father, Spirit, Son;
> In God, new life is begun.
>
> Together as the Church, we pray,
> for this child's future from today;
> For health and happiness and joy,

for new life as a child of God.
Help us to share peace, truth and love,
Gifts of God, given from above.

The Baptism Liturgy

REV. GAYLE TAYLOR

This baptism liturgy was put together using parts from Common Order *(Saint Andrew Press, 1994 edn, pp. 83, 84) but other original words too. Theologically, the act has demonstrated that this sacrament is about what God does for us regardless of what we do for God. It is a declaration of his unconditional love.*

We hear these words from the Gospel according to Matthew 28:18–30 (NIV):

Jesus said:

> 'Full authority on heaven and earth has been committed to me. Go therefore to all nations and make them my disciples; baptise them in the name of the Father and the Son and the Holy Spirit, and teach them to observe all that I have commanded you. And I will be with you always, to the end of time.'

And, in the Gospel according to Luke 18:16–17 (NIV), we hear of a time when some people brought their children for Jesus to bless and the disciples scolded them, but Jesus called for the children and said:

> 'Let the children come to me; do not try to stop them; for the kingdom of God belongs to such as these. Truly I tell you: whoever does not accept the kingdom of God like a child will never enter it.'

Jesus Christ is with us in this baptism today; it is he himself who baptises us, and by the Holy Spirit we are brought into his Church.

In this sacrament, the love of God is offered to each one of us. Though we cannot fully understand or explain it, we are called to accept that love with the openness and trust of a child.

Let us pray:

Loving God, you are the maker and giver of life, and we thank you this morning for the journey of all our days where we can learn more of you and begin to experience your great love for us. We especially thank you today for little N ... and for the joy and blessing he / she has brought to the whole family circle. At key moments in our life, we are often more fully aware of your presence, and today we come together because we recognise your hand at work bringing us beyond anxiety and confusion to deep joy and meaning. Father, we confess this morning that at times you have not meant all that you should to us because we have closed ourselves off, focused on other things and chosen other ways; but you give us a fresh start through your gracious gifts of water and the Holy Spirit in baptism.

Throughout time, you have communicated your love and blessings through water, and on this day we come to touch your child N ... with water that is a visible sign of a new beginning in you. Father God, we thank you for family today, for support and care, acceptance and the feeling of belonging, because we affirm our belief at this time in your family, Christ's body the Church: where all are welcome, where small beginnings lead to firm commitments, where promises are made on the basis of potential, and love abounds through your goodness and grace.

May the sacrament of your grace and visible signs of your goodness today lead us all into a deeper realisation of your love ever waiting for us and your power beyond our understanding.

Transforming God, send your Holy Spirit upon us and this water through Jesus Christ our Lord, and hear us as we pray together the family prayer that he taught us:

Our Father ...

Parent(s) or sponsors are invited to bring the child forward.

Full Name ... I baptise you, in the name of the Father and of the Son and of the Holy Spirit and with the Christian name/s ... The Lord bless you and keep you.

N ... for you Jesus Christ came into the world, for you he lived and showed God's love, for you he suffered the darkness of Calvary and cried at the last: 'It is accomplished', for you he triumphed over death and rose in newness of life; for you he ascended to reign at God's right hand. All this he did for you, *N ...* though you do not know it yet. And so the word of Scripture is fulfilled: 'We love because God loved us first'.

God's love does not depend on anything we do; it is unconditional. We love because God loved us first, and so in response to that love we all have a part to play in *N's ...* baptism today.

N ... and N ... as *N's* parents will you please respond to these questions:

Having presented your child for baptism, desiring that she may be grafted into Christ as a member of his body, the Church, do you confess your faith in God the Father and in his Son Jesus Christ as your Saviour and Lord?

I do.

And do you promise, depending on the grace of God, to teach your child the truths and duties of the Christian faith and by prayer and example to bring her up in the life and worship of the Church?

I do.

Your child now belongs to God in Christ. From this day, she will be at home in the Christian community and there will always be a place for her here and in the wider Church throughout the world.

As a sign of all of this, *N* ..., the family elder, will now come forward to welcome *N* ... into the arms of the Church, and as a congregation we make our promise to *N* ... and to God.

Could the congregation please stand? Could you repeat after me:

N ..., we welcome you into our church family,

We are members together of the body of Christ.

We are children of the one God.

We affirm our faith in God our creator, in Jesus our saviour, in the Holy Spirit our guide.

We accept our responsibilities to encourage you, and all other children in our midst, to grow up in the knowledge and love of Christ.

N ..., we welcome you.

We sing the blessing 'The Lord bless you and keep you' (hymn 796, *CH4*).

Please be seated.

N ..., one of our children from the church family has flowers from the Sunday school for *N's* ... mum on this special day for the whole family.

Let us pray:

God of love, we rejoice again to receive your grace in word and sacrament.

We have heard your call and are made new by your Spirit.
Continue to guide and guard *N ...* all her days,
may your love hold her, your truth guide her, your joy
delight her.
Bless her parents *N... and N...* and big brother/s/sister/s; wee
brother/s/sisters
that he/she may grow up in a secure and happy home
and give to her/his godparents *N ... and N ...,* and to the
whole family, wisdom and courage,
laughter and peace, and love that endures all things.
God of grace, in whose holy catholic Church there is one Lord,
one faith, one baptism,
help us to acknowledge that Jesus Christ is Lord,
to profess with our whole lives the one true faith,
and to live in love and unity with all who are baptised in
his name,
through Jesus Christ our Lord,
who lives and reigns with you, Father, and the Holy Spirit
one God for ever and ever.   Amen.

Thanksgiving for the Gift of a Child

REV. EVIE YOUNG

Introduction

(Parents and baby, along with any other siblings, join minister on chancel)

Today, we are glad to have with us in this service of worship baby N and his/her parents X and Y Z, who are part of this congregation.

Having come to our Church family from another tradition of the Christian Church, and having given careful thought and consideration to bringing their new baby for baptism, they have concluded that they want to leave the decision about baptism to be made by their baby once he/she is old enough to make his/her own response to the love of God in Jesus Christ.

Today, X and Y have not brought N for baptism,
But they have brought him/her

- as an act of thanksgiving to God, recognising that he/she is a precious gift, entrusted by God to them.

They have brought him/her

- to receive God's blessing, as mothers long ago brought their children to Jesus, who took them in his arms and blessed them.

They have brought him/her

- to be among God's people in this place, where together our Christian witness creates a community of faith in which children can learn to know Jesus Christ.

Scripture says:
Jesus called for the children and said, 'Let the children come to me; do not try to stop them; for the kingdom of God belongs to such as these. Truly I tell you: whoever does not accept the kingdom of God like a child will never enter it.'
(Luke 18:16–17, REB)

Prayer

Let us pray.

Gracious God our Father,

We praise you for all your gifts to us.

Especially this day, we give thanks for your gift of baby N to his/her family, and now to us, his/her family in faith.

We thank you for giving us the honour and responsibility of caring for young lives and teaching them about you. We thank you for their joy and liveliness, enthusiasm and affection – signs of your own Spirit and love.

Thanks be to you in Jesus' name.   AMEN.

Presentation

(Minister takes baby)

N, all around you now are God's family – people who love Jesus Christ and try to follow him.

We are so delighted to have you here among us.

People of God, meet baby *N*. Welcome him/her in Jesus' name and care for him/her with all Christian kindliness and grace.

Dedication of Parents

X and *Y* will now ask God's help as parents.

Parents say together:

God our Father, we thank you for the gift of baby *N*.

Help us to live together as a family in love, joy and peace.

Give us wisdom to be good parents that we may love and serve you faithfully, through Jesus Christ our Lord.   AMEN.

(Minister returns baby to parents)

Blessing

Let us pray:

Gracious God,

We ask your blessing on baby *N*, on his/her parents, (brother/s/sister/s) and their home.

And may they always walk in your ways and to your glory.

Through Jesus Christ our Lord.   AMEN.

Section 2
Weddings

A Wedding Talk on Trust

REV. SHIRLEY FRASER

This contribution is a wedding address, which is printed off to give to newly-weds, often with the gift of a Bible. I have received many positive comments on an address that is short and easily remembered.

- John 2:1–11: Jesus at the wedding in Cana
- Mary's trust in her son that he would respond to her plea
- The servants' trust in Jesus' order
- The bridegroom's trust in the evidence before his eyes: that a miracle had taken place.

TRUST in the marriage relationship:

T is for TRUTHFULNESS. That means working hard at open, honest, real communication, especially at a feeling level.

R is for RESPECT. That is such an essential quality in a good marriage, because to respect the other is to value him or her very highly, and to want to be utterly loyal, throughout life together.

U is for UNSELFISHNESS. It may be as practical as asking one another daily: 'What would you like? What can I do to show my love for you? What can we do together to share our lives and our home with others?'

S is for SENSITIVITY. That is about learning to interpret the subtle, unspoken cues which we give to one another; about noticing each other's smallest needs. It may be reflected in the frequency with which we use expressions such as 'I love you', 'I am here for you' and 'I am sorry', or 'I was wrong'.

T is for THOUGHTFULNESS. Love is far more than just a wonderful feeling. Love is an attitude of mind. As we think lovingly, so we will act lovingly.

Proverbs 3:5–7

> *TRUST in the LORD:* vital foundation for marriage and all living.

Marriage was Invented by God

REV. MARJORY MacLEAN

These statements slot in among the more traditional words of the three Orders for Marriage in Common Order, *pages 195–224.**

- Marriage was invented by God so that people could be friends in the most profound of ways, and make the world a more noble place by their example.

- Marriage was invented by God so that people could be lovers and teach the world lessons of tenderness that this tired earth desperately needs to learn.

- Marriage was invented by God so that people could become families … and perhaps one day share their lives with children … on loan from heaven.

or, where it is not appropriate to anticipate the birth of children, and if either party has children already,

- Marriage was invented by God as a basis for family life, sometimes for very young new families but just as importantly as a place of welcome and refuge for families that already exist.

---

* *Book of Common Order*, 3rd edn (Edinburgh: Saint Andrew Press, 2005), ISBN 978 0 7152 0830 4.

A Silver Wedding Ceremony

REV. LYNN BRADY

This liturgy grew out of the desire of friends of mine to go back to the church they were married in twenty-five years earlier and reflect on the personal journey of marriage. Though it is very personal to them, I hope it will help others to reflect on their anniversary and write their own liturgy.

Introduction: spoken by either wife or husband.

Twenty-five years ago, we came to this building, and in the presence of God and our closest friends and family we declared our love for each other and made a commitment to love each other for the rest of our days. At that time, we sang the hymn 'Christ is made the sure foundation, Christ the head and cornerstone'. That foundation is as sure to us now as it was then, and we wanted to come together in this place again to give thanks for what has been and to renew the vows that we made to each other before God and before our friends. Our relationship has not existed in a vacuum. We were born of love, and our families first showed us love and taught us how to love, and we are the people we are today because of them. Our friends have journeyed with us, old friends and new friends, who have loved and supported us and who have allowed us to love them in return. We are so grateful for that, and hope you will continue on this journey with us. May this short time today affirm our friendship and commitment to each other, and may you all find blessing through these words.

Reading: Ephesians 3:14–21

Prayer of thanks for what has been, by yourself if that's suitable (including for health, happiness, and for never having been wanting in any respect).

Prayer of thanks for husband and wife
> Life-giver, Pain-bearer, Love-maker,
> O Lord our God, how wonderful is life!
> > How rich its variety of joy and sorrow!
> > How precious are the lives of those dear to us!
> > > Life is *your* gift,
> In everything that makes life worth living,
> > it's you we see at work.
> In every human life we see something of you
> And, in the end, it's only in you that our lives make sense.
> Living God, we praise you for the gift of life!
> > The life of our friends N ... and N ...
> > whom you have touched and shaped with your own
> > hands.

> O Lord our God, how glorious is love!
> > How wonderful are the various aspects of love we've
> > seen:
> > > in the parents who brought us into this world,
> > > in the family and friends who have cared for
> > > us;
> > > and especially today we celebrate the love of
> > > N ... and N ...
> > > > the love they have for you, Loving God,
> > > > and the love they have for each other.
> Love is your presence.
> > It's you we know, when we know love;
> > It's you we see reflected in everybody who loves us.
> We thank you for all N ... and N ... have shared together
> and with others;

the love that they have shared with the many friends
old and new
they have journeyed with over the last twenty-five
years.

Loving God, we praise you for the gift of love today!
Love that brought [*children's names may be mentioned here*]
into the world,
and your sustaining love that has been part of their
shaping.
It's you whose love will never let us go, it's your
love that forgives;
It's your love that enables us to endure the hard
times, sad times.
It's your love that keeps us going, keeps us trying,
when things are tough.
Lord, on this day, may life and love be renewed in us all,
and especially in N ... and N ... so that the love
that joined their lives together twenty-five years
ago may continue to be truly your spirit working
through them.

May life and love pour into our lives now ...
light up all that we are doing with a new glory,
so that we may know your presence.
May it be your love that enables them to reaffirm their
vows
and to keep them for as long as they both shall
live.   AMEN.

Thank you

*This will be a few short sentences by both husband and wife
thanking each other for what he/she has given to the other. (Not
to be revealed to one another before the service!)*

Vows

> *The couple are encouraged to create their own.*

Reading

> *Chosen by the couple and read by a younger member of the family if possible.*

Short comment

> *From the minister about what it means to be real!*

Apache Blessing

> *Said by wife and husband.*

A Celtic Blessing *by the minister*

> May the raindrops fall lightly upon your brow,
> May the soft winds freshen your spirit,
> May the sunshine brighten your heart,
> May the burden of the day rest lightly upon you
> And may God enfold you in the mantle of his love.

> Thank you both for all your sharing, laughing and listening.
> For your comforting, supporting and shielding .
> Your forgiving, trusting and respecting.
> Your honouring, cherishing and loving.

> May God continue to bless you both as you travel on together.

Section 3
Loss and Remembrance

My Miscarriage

REV. ROSIE FREW

I do believe that honesty and vulnerability are important facets of ministry. When we open ourselves up to others, they respond, and we have the privilege and the pain of sharing their deepest hopes and fears and sharing also the love and compassion of Christ.

In my final year at university, I had to write a dissertation. One of the subjects I covered in it was miscarriage, in particular the pastoral care of those who had experienced this loss of a pregnancy. I remember being very moved as I did my research and read account after account of personal heartbreak. I hoped that my study would give me an understanding and empathy in my future ministry.

Over the years, I've spent time with a number of women who have miscarried. And then, sadly, at the beginning of July, when I was twelve weeks pregnant, I experienced the pain of miscarriage for myself. I can now speak from a very personal perspective.

People were very kind and thoughtful. With cards and flowers, they wanted to show that they shared our sorrow and disappointment. People, unknowingly, were also very hurtful. '*You* must have been working too hard. *You* must have been lifting things. *You* can't have been taking care of yourself properly.' The medical profession will tell you that miscarriage is a very common event – it is rarely anyone's fault, there is usually no obvious reason 'why?' I had no cause to feel guilty, and I knew that, yet blame was being apportioned to me. Others, again unthinkingly, all too easily dismissed our loss as trivial. 'You're young, you can try again, the fun's in the trying ...' The loss of a pregnancy is the loss of dreams and hopes and possibilities, and the loss of a child that has been very real and yet hidden.

Miscarriage has been described as the loneliest grief. There is not always, on the part of others, a full appreciation of, and respect for, the powerful feelings of loss and bereavement that are usually engendered. I've had to learn that the hard way, not just from books in a library.

I thank God that I have a healthy, happy, boisterous almost-two-year-old, and I pray that in the future he will have a brother or sister. However, the 2nd of February will always be remembered as the day when the baby we lost was due to have been born.

> My frame was not hidden from you
> when I was made in the secret place.
> When I was woven together in the depths of the earth,
> your eyes saw my unformed body.
> All the days ordained for me
> were written in your book
> before one of them came to be. (Psalm 139, NIV)

Following this article, a number of women wrote to me to share their stories of loss and to offer me comfort in my loss – some heartbreaking stories of repeated miscarriage and feelings of failure and desperation. As I went about my parish, several women spoke to me of their own experiences and thanked me for 'speaking out' on their behalf.

My story has a happy ending. My daughter, Rebecca, was born in June 1998. Following my announcement of my pregnancy to my congregation, an elderly lady asked me to visit her. With tears pouring down her cheeks, she told me that she too had had a miscarriage when her only daughter was two but, despite her husband being desperate for a second child, she had felt unable to face the possibility of another heartbreak. Their loss and her decision remained a tension between them throughout their married life. She ended by saying: 'I so wish I had had your courage', by which time my tears were flowing too.

A Funeral for a Baby Girl

REV. LIZ CRUMLISH

This contribution was used at the funeral of a baby girl when I was a hospital chaplain. This service celebrated a life, albeit a brief life. I think the words come from a mother's heart.

Emma was a beautiful baby girl born with Edwards' syndrome. She lived for fourteen months and brought lots of joy to those who had the privilege of meeting her. As hospital chaplain, I encountered Emma and her parents a lot and helped them plan her funeral service:

> 'I will never forget you, … I have written your name on the palms of my hands.' (Isaiah 49:15–16, GNB)

We are here today to share with Emma's mum and dad in their great loss. We're here, not to tell them that everything will be OK. For how can it ever be?

But we are here just to be with them and with their families at this time when nothing makes any sense, when there are no explanations, no answers. Let us pray.

> God of love, love is your gift to us; love to give, to receive, to share.
> Love can bring the deepest joy but also the keenest suffering.

We suffer today because we loved so much, because of the
joy brought to us by Emma's brief presence. We can't
even pretend to understand.

But we pray that you understand us, you, who knew and
felt the pain of others, surround us with yet more of that
love you give.

And help us, even in our darkness, to give thanks for the
love which Emma awakened in us.

May we know that, as she brought so much to our lives,
she remains your child forever.

Today, may we feel her presence and yours and
be assured that that love can never be taken from us.

Be with us now as we pay these last offices of love in this
place, through Christ our Lord.   Amen.

Reading

We read an excerpt from *Winnie the Pooh* by A. A. Milne
– a time when the friends were struggling to say
goodbye.

Committal

God gives life, and God takes it away.

And the taking away is so terribly painful, because what
he gives is so very good.

Emma, you are one of God's children, held forever in love.

May the Lord bless you and keep you.

May the Lord be kind and gracious to you.

May the Lord smile upon you and give you
peace.

Sleep in the sleep of all calm. Sleep in the sleep of all loves.

Sleep, beloved Emma, in the God of life.

Let us pray.

God of life, we thank you that we do not belong only to
ourselves but to one another.

Our lives are woven together in care, in tenderness, in
    hope to a pattern we do not yet understand.
Sorrow and sadness can bind us closer still as we discover
    a shared strength,
                a deeper, more mysterious love.
In and through their shared and bitter grief, may Emma's
    parents come to feel this to be true.
May they be sure that Emma's life continues to be woven
    into theirs
            and that all is held together by love.
May they know what good and loving parents they are
    and how much they have given to Emma.
Help them to comfort one another, not to withdraw into
    themselves,
            but to talk often and to care for one another.
We pray too for their families.
Give them comfort, your courage and your strength
    through all that lies ahead.
Thank you for all the support they have known already,
            from each other, from neighbours, from friends.
Help all of us here to support one another and to come to
    know, in time,
            the depth of your support, the breadth of your
                loving arms around us.
We ask this in the name of Christ who died for us. Amen.

Jesus said: Peace I give to you, peace such as the world
    cannot give.
Set your troubled hearts at rest and banish your fears.
Christ's peace be with us as we go on our way this day
    and forever.   Amen.

Resting Place

REV. GILLEAN MACLEAN

This poem was written after the scattering of ashes on Iona of a member of my congregation who had come to faith on that island. I use poetry often in worship – my own and others'. I think that, as we try to express what is essentially mystery, often it is only in poetry that we can come close to an understanding. Some of the best poetry I have read is by women. The mistress of the love poem, after all, is surely Christina Rossetti. She wrote about love, human love, but also about divine love and how the two are inextricably linked.

'Resting Place'
Here,
in this place
to dance with seagulls
over white-tipped waves,
to sing with the curlew
the corncrake and the skylark
to swim with the seals
through forests of swaying kelp.
Freed,
at the last
from the restrictions of the earth
the vagaries of time
the restraints of the years.

One with tides and seasons
an eternal jewelled droplet
part of the endless breath of God.
And yet,
not resting at all
ever moving, changing, creating.
Finished with life.
Alive to eternity.

Loss, Love and Growth

REV. ALISON HUTCHISON

This was used in small church-group and hospital settings. It allows the acknowledging and addressing of the pain of various kinds of loss and the hope of growth through them, with God's help.

Loss

Leader

It has been said that life begins in loss – in the very act of birth, we lose the comfort and security of our mother's womb and are forced out to face a strange and unfamiliar world. The act of birth is inseparable from the pain of letting go. That experience of loss and new birth continues life-long.

When we think of loss, we tend to think of the aching grief of losing a loved one in death. However, loss plays a larger part in our lives. We leave places and people, and are left by them. We may lose opportunities or our dreams, our hopes. There are times we lose our identities, or the person we long to be. We may lose our health suddenly or slowly as we age. We may know the loss and grief of being separated from each other by distance or disagreement.

Let us acknowledge our losses and the grief they bring ...

Reflective prayer

To be spoken by one or more people. Explain that silence will be used.

Voice 1

Living, loving God, we bring to you now any loss, any grief, large or small, deserved or undeserved, expected or unexpected. (*pause*)

Voice 2

We have lost those we loved, Lord – death, disagreement or distance separate us. Our lives have changed, for they are no longer with us. We are grateful for the loves shared, yet deeply mourn their absence. In the midst of our grief, past and present, you know and understand the confusion of our many different thoughts and feelings. We lift those thoughts and feelings to you now. (*Silence – at least ten seconds*)

Voice 3

We may lose our health, Lord. We feel cheated as body and mind fail us. We may face restricted lives, and the shackles of our times of ill-health are irksome and heavy. We lift our thoughts and feelings to you now. (*Silence – at least ten seconds*)

Voice 4

We may have lost ourselves, Lord, the people we long to be. We are unsure of who we are, how we should live, and have lost our way. We lift our thoughts and feelings to you now. (*Silence – at least ten seconds*)

Leader

Suffering Lord, share our pain and give us courage. Healing God, take our grief and ease its ache. May your great love, and the love of those around us, be the balm for grief past, the strength for living today and the hope for our future. Amen.

Love

Leader

Whatever we suffer in life, let us remember the love which never leaves us.

Reader

Who shall separate us from the love of Christ? Shall trouble or hardship or persecution or famine or nakedness or danger or sword? No, in all things we are more than conquerors through him who loved us. For I am convinced that neither death, nor life, neither angels nor demons, neither the present nor the future, nor any powers, neither height nor depth, nor anything else in all creation, will be able to separate us from the love of God that is in Christ Jesus our Lord. (Romans 8:35, 37–9, NIV)

Growth

Leader

Only crushed wheat can be made into bread. Only trampled grapes can be made into wine. Loss may crush our lives and grief may trample our spirits, but love and courage can transform them.

We have the choice. We can remain in our hurt, or with divine and human help we can accept, adapt and grow. Even in the most devastating loss we can find the opportunity to create something new, so that the loss need not be futile. As the act of birth is inseparable from the pain of letting go, we can find new birth and growth.

The Rainbow Tree

REV. CATRIONA OGILVIE

Each year, about two Sundays before Christmas, the 'Rainbow Tree' starts the service as a bare branch cemented into a tub. During the service, people come forward and tie a ribbon on the tree, one for each person they wish to remember. The ribbons are of all the colours of the rainbow – red, orange, yellow, green, blue, indigo and violet – to remind all of God's promises seen in the rainbow.

The tree stays in the church until Easter, when the ribbons are removed and sewn into something for the church.

This whole act reaches a very deep need, because bereaved people find the 'jolly' side of Christmas so hard. Many churches hold similar services using small candles for remembrance; but we have found the lasting nature of the ribbons, and the fact they are kept and used year by year, to be especially appreciated.

The tree itself can be viewed on Cumbernauld Old Parish Church website along with some of the things that have been made with each year's ribbons.

Prayer

> May the light of Christ shining through our tears
> become the rainbow of Your promise;
> shining colours of Your love's bright presence
> in Your grieving, struggling, yet hoping world. (Anon.)

RAF Remembrance Day Service

REV. CAROLINE TAYLOR

St Athernase Church in Leuchars has as its neighbour RAF Leuchars. This prayer was shared at a joint Remembrance Day service at which RAF personnel and their families were present as well as ex-Air Force and Army personnel and civilians.

Photographs

> In frames on the mantelpiece or bedside table
> Attached by magnets to the fridge
> Sent by e-mail

So many photographs, Lord, all of them depicting people who are loved.

Photographs

> of men and women in uniform of a style which betrays
> that they weren't taken yesterday
> of recent passing-out parades showing the optimism and
> confidence of youth
> jet, ship or tank, bleak desert, icy mountain or ruined city
> in the background.
> Combat gear, khaki, Air Force blue, number 1s, off-duty
> casual

So many photographs, Lord, all of them depicting people who are loved.

And today we remember those whose photographs we treasure because of the good memories they evoke, even as we sigh for what might have been:

> Those who went to war and didn't come home;
> those who came back but not as we had known them;
> those who met their deaths on the home front;
> those who struggle still to live with their battle scars,
>   emotional or physical.

May your love surround them all, dear God.

And we remember women, children and men in the thick of conflict even as we pray. Keep them safe.

This morning, we include in our prayers the waiting ones at home; those who live daily with the worry of what might happen. For the children who are too young to understand but who know the military life of a father or mother. Surround them all with your peace, Lord.

And we pray for ourselves, dear God, that we, who bear your Son's name, may be channels of your peace; that the Church be a sign of hope in a divided world.

Like those who have given themselves in the service of their country, we give ourselves to your service, wholeheartedly for the sake of our Lord Jesus Christ in whose name we offer these prayers. Amen.

Memorial Stones

REV. DOROTHY ANDERSON

I wrote this memorial piece because I couldn't find anything in this area of ministry that was particularly helpful in a non-religious context.

We probably all know the various ways we can use stones and pebbles symbolically. This is a version of an Act of Remembrance I took for a group of largely non-churchgoers who wanted to do something to mark the death by suicide of their colleague, a man in his late thirties.

Before the service, at the front of the worship space (or other accessible spot), place a rug or other covering. In the middle, place four or five large stones (available from garden centres).

As the congregation gathers, give them each a small polished stone. Try to make them of different sizes, colours, types (these too can be obtained from garden centres, where they are cheaper than those found in gift shops – but they tend to come in bulk!).

At the appropriate moment, explain:

When you came in, you were given/chose a stone. Look at them now. No two are alike – they are different sizes, shapes, colours and so on. Just as we are.

Yet we are all connected through *AB* who has died. For in his/her living and in his/her dying, he/she has affected us and brings us together now.

In front of me are some stones – the start not of a cairn *[I thought of building a cairn but the thought of the symbolism if it collapsed put me off!]* but of a pattern. I don't know what pattern – that is up to you.

Each of us can come and place our stone down – wherever you want. Where you put it will affect the pattern, and may influence someone else's decision. But together we create the bigger picture. It needs all of us together, united despite our differences, and our individual contributions to create the pattern.

As you come forward, feel the stone in your hand, think about its size and shape. As you lay it down, think about *AB* and what he/she means to you. As you lay the stone down, it is your act of remembrance but also your release.

Use the laying down of the stone as a way of letting go also of any burdens you are carrying. Of remorse, guilt, anger, hurt, pain.

And as you return to your places, note that your hands are empty; you are no longer carrying that stone. You return slightly lighter than when you came – use the space left by the stone and by the laying down of your burdens as a chink to let in the light, as an openness to help and healing and wholeness.

NB: Some people may prefer to take their stone as a memento. That is OK – the fact that their stone is not laid down affects the pattern too.

Closure of Deerness West Church: 16 October 1994

REV. JOAN CRAIG

At the closure of the former Deerness West Church in Orkney, the status and use of buildings were and are contentious and painful issues in this part of the world. The service of closure acknowledged the pain but also the creativity and faith of the members in moving on with grace and thanksgiving – and to be a stimulus to other ministers and members trying to make meaning and note of a painful moment in their church's history.

Flower festival and thanksgiving service

Opening
Who is able to build a house for God when heaven itself, the highest heaven, cannot contain him?

Prayer
God of love and power, you hold all souls in life. You bind together all your people in heaven and earth in one holy fellowship. We praise you for those who in their generation have been lights in the world, in this church and parish. We thank you for their courage and commitment, for their vision and generosity in establishing this place of worship. Help us to keep faith with them and their vision, through Jesus Christ our Lord.   Amen.

Sermon: Disruption and Reunion

The Disruption of the Church of Scotland in 1843 was the result of complex issues. The focus of concern was the system of patronage by which the landowners chose and appointed parish ministers. Government resisted the growing demand for the right of congregations to choose their own minister, and for the Church to be free from state control over its affairs. Things came to a head in March 1843 when the House of Commons rejected an appeal to consider the grievances of the Church concerning Patronage and the Claim of Right to spiritual independence. When the General Assembly of the Church of Scotland met on 18 May, the retiring Moderator, Professor David Welsh, read out a protest and led some 200 ministers and elders out of the Assembly. They then constituted themselves 'The Church of Scotland – Free'. The Disruption had taken place, and the Free Church was born.

This was a most important event in Scottish church history, involving considerable financial and social sacrifices for the sake of principles. Ministers and people had to face the financial demands of building up their denomination out of nothing. The Deerness West Church came into being as a result of the dynamic growth of the Free Church.

There are four remarkable results of the Disruption that I want to mention.

The first was the great liberality of people up and down the country. It was a new thing for the Church to depend entirely on the voluntary contributions of members.

The second was the commitment to serve the needs of the whole Church. Local congregational liberality enabled important social work to be undertaken, highly respected theological colleges to be established, and the development of extensive mission work overseas.

The third was the revival of worship. Ordinary services contained only a couple of praise items, taken from the metrical psalms or paraphrases. There was no organ or other instrumental accompaniment. Singing was led by the precentor, and usually only a handful of tunes were used. With the revival, choirs were formed, hymnbooks introduced, and the battle in favour of an organ was eventually won. Many churches were gutted, reconstructed to a better standard, and made places of beauty with fine furnishings.

Fourthly, organisations grew up: the Woman's and Men's Guilds, the Sunday School, Bible classes, Work Parties and so on. The Church was no longer a place to which people came to sit and listen to sermons. It was becoming a place where people did things, discussed their faith, and witnessed to it by taking part in practical service to others.

Unfortunately, the Disruption resulted also in bitterness and strife. Hard things were said on both sides. Personal friendships were destroyed. Nevertheless, there was a genuine longing on both sides for reunion. In due course, Parliament did acknowledge the freedom of the Church of Scotland to order its own spiritual life and work. The way opened up for reconciliation and for Union in 1929. Part of the driving force towards union was the deep desire to meet responsibilities more effectively and less wastefully as partners rather than as rivals. Readjustment has been going on slowly since then throughout Scotland, with parishes and congregations uniting, and numbers of ministers and of church buildings being reduced. What we are doing today is part of that process that has been going on up and down the land for most of the past century.

We are keeping faith with our forebears who began the work of this church. We hope that this consolidation of our resources at St Ninian's will enable us to play our part in the wider work of the Church more effectively. In joining hands with our neighbours in St Andrew's and Holm, we seek to strengthen and enliven our fellowship in worship and service. We thank God that the divisions and hurts of the past have been healed. Here in Deerness today, we are expressing this most fully as we centre our life together in St Ninian's.

Declaration of closure

It is not necessary for us to have two buildings in this parish. It is necessary for us in exercise of good stewardship and for the better service of God and of the wider Church to close one of them.

God has built his Church on the foundation of the apostles and prophets, saints and martyrs, on the obedience of Mary, the faithfulness of Andrew, the missionary zeal of Ninian and Drostan.

Christ Jesus is the cornerstone. We are the living stones of his Church – a spiritual house, a holy priesthood, called to offer spiritual sacrifices acceptable to God.

Believing this,

> in obedience to the instructions of the General Assembly
>   and of the Presbytery of Orkney,
> in accordance with the decision of this congregation,
> and trusting in the living God,

I now declare this church to be closed as a place for worship.

Prayer

Lord Jesus, you are before us, beckoning us, directing us, challenging us. We sorrow as we leave this place. Help us to believe in your new and risen life for us as individuals and as a congregation. Light of the world, be light for our journey of faith as we go forth in your name.

Lighting of the candles

As we sing the next hymn ('One more step along the world I go'), please come forward and light your candle. Keep it lit until after the close of service. Let the lighting of your candle from this central one be to you a sign and symbol, that as you go from here, you take something with you from this place which will be within you: the light of Christ for your life and for the life of the world.

Benediction

> You are God's temple,
>> where the spirit of God dwells.
> May he keep you sound in faith,
>> steadfast in hope, strong in love.
> The peace of God remain in this place.
> The peace of God be within us as we leave this place.
> The peace of God which we have found in this place go
>> with us in our hearts.
>> And the blessing of God almighty,
>> Father, Son and Holy Spirit,
>> be with you all.   Amen.

Section 4
Pastoral Care

Home but Not Forgotten

REV. JILL CLANCY

This material reminds us of the importance of those who are still part of the Church but who are unable to attend any longer, usually the housebound. I feel that ordained women can have a special bond with older women.

During my training as a minister, when I worked at home in Fullarton Church and in Castlemilk, one of the things that I developed while at both of those churches was something I call 'Home but Not Forgotten'. As you know, there are many of our members who are unable to be with us due to unforeseen circumstances and mainly just because they are a little older and frailer than they used to be when they took an active part in church life and faith. And so, during the week, I went along to meet with what I think must be one of the oldest members of St John's, Mrs Jessie Spence, who is 98 years of age – and I asked her a few questions.

The first question I asked her was *what were her memories of church*, and this is what she shared with us. She said that her first memory of church was going to the Bay Mission in Manor Crescent when she was a wee girl. She remembers getting a penny for the collection, and she had to be sure to put it in.

She also remembers that, every time she went to the wee mission, she would get a golden text from her teacher, and if she managed to get twelve by the end of the year she got a prize, and the one that Jessie remembers is the book *What Katy Did*.

She also remembers the Guildry play that she was in which was held at the Bethany Hall, and she remembers how as a wee girl she thought she was wonderful, but her mum was embarrassed because she kept wanting to be in the front row even though she was the smallest.

I then asked Jessie *what was her typical Sunday?* She told me that they only wore their best clothes on a Sunday, and in her family Dad would take them out for a walk in the hills first, then after dinner they went along to the Sunday School about 4pm, and once she got bigger she went to the Bible Class which was led by Mr and Mrs Johnstone, who were missionaries. And then they had an evening service about 7pm.

Jessie also remembers the Sunday School trips, going to Blairmore with a 'tinny' round her neck. And there they would have teas and races before going back home on the steamer.

Jessie loved church and was a great attender in her young days, as even the milkman commented on how her family got all the prizes and no-one else got a look in.

I then asked Jessie what her *best memories of her active time at St John's were*. She said it was when she got married around 18 years of age that she got involved in St John's, which was eighty years ago. She enjoyed her days here, worshipping faithfully every Sunday and enjoying the indoor bowling and for some time the Tuesday afternoons at the Guild. She also said that she enjoyed the Christmas dances in the church hall.

Then I asked Jessie *if her faith had been tried and tested down through the years.* And she told me that she felt fortunate all her life, but when her first husband Steven Baird died it was the worst time of her life. But she can now say without a doubt that God saw her through that time and has kept her strong.

I then finally asked Jessie if she had a favourite hymn or Bible passage that she would like to share with us today. She told me a few favourite hymns, but the one that has been going round and round in her head all week, she said, was 'This is my story', or what is also known as 'Blessed assurance'.

Then she also shared with me that during this time of Easter she has been thinking a lot about Mary, Jesus' mother, and how Mary had to watch her son die and could do nothing to help him. Jessie's son Bill lives many miles away in England, and at this moment he is looking after his wife, who is frail and unwell. Jessie wishes that she didn't have to just look on but could help, so in some respects she is feeling with a greater understanding how Mary must have felt to watch helpless as her son took on the sins of the world.

Today, folks, I have shared with you some special thoughts and memories from a special lady, Mrs Jessie Spence; and I hope, as we pray for her and sing one of her favourite hymns today, that she will know that she may be at home but that she is not forgotten.

Preparing for God?

REV. LIZ CRUMLISH

Eileen was an elderly medical patient decanted to a surgical ward because no place could be found for her in a nursing home. She was known by that awful term so fashionable for a time – a bed-blocker. Our relationship had grown over many weeks. She was referred to me while she awaited psychiatric assessment to determine whether or not she was clinically depressed. The verdict returned that she was not clinically depressed but just 'a miserable old lady'. This was interpreted by ward staff as 'a challenge for the chaplain'.

It was no wonder Eileen was miserable. Still grieving the loss of her husband, who had died just nine months before, she was, in a relatively short space of time, deemed unable to live on her own. Going to live with family was not an option. She was bereft and bewildered. It took a considerable time to elicit this information; but, during that time, glimpses of the capable lady who had spent her life running a hostel for young men emerged. She was a feisty, formidable yet gentle woman. While waiting on a more suitable place becoming available, she succumbed to an inevitable hospital infection and rapidly deteriorated. I would often get a call from her ward at some ungodly hour asking that I come and see her. She was lonely and frightened. Once in the middle of the night, as I sat holding her hand, feeling a bit useless and hoping she would drop off to sleep, I asked her: 'Are you sure there is nothing I can do for you?' To which she replied: 'Would you shave my chin?'

Chaplains will tell you there is nothing to which they cannot turn their hands. I was soon armed with a razor and soothing cream. As I attended to her bristles, we both had tears rolling down our cheeks. She said: 'You have just done a very Christ-like thing'.

I didn't see Eileen again. She died shortly after that. But I always felt that shaving an old lady's bristles was much more sacred than any prayer or other religious offering I might have made.

And I like to think that her welcome into heaven was all the smoother because of that encounter in the wee small hours.

We never know when we will get the opportunity to be Christ to one another. And that opportunity can present itself in some of the most bizarre scenarios. It calls for no special language or liturgy but simply a willingness to look into each other's eyes and see Christ present.

Free to Belong

REV. ROSEMARY LEGGE

The theme of this sermon is 'Freedom'. This is a subject that many people can relate to. It is based on the freedom that Jesus brought to the women of his day. 2008 is the ruby anniversary of the ordination of women in the Church of Scotland; and, when this piece was written in 2007, that year marked the 200th anniversary of the abolition of slavery, hence the themes of women and freedom.

READING: Mark 5:21–34

Illustration

I have a book called *What Our Grandmothers Knew,* and in it are instructions for a face pack: 'Collect pumpkin, cucumber and melon seeds. Sponge them carefully between blotting paper, dry them away from sunlight and then grind them to a powder. Take a dessertspoon of each and mix into a thick cream by adding milk. Apply the cream to your face and leave it on for about half and hour. Wipe off carefully. Rinse your face in lukewarm water and massage in some rose-water.'

Evidently, years ago, some people went to a lot of trouble with face packs, hoping to stay young and beautiful. And things haven't changed. Some people still go to a lot of trouble and expense with face packs and creams, hoping to stay young and beautiful. But in fact there is more to keeping skin looking young and healthy than simply putting on face cream. Our skin has a layer called collagen just below the surface, which keeps skin soft, and this needs plenty of vitamin C. So a healthy diet with lots of fresh green vegetables and citrus fruit will probably do more for your skin than any expensive cream. It is not enough to treat only the surface; we need to deal with the underlying needs also.

And so it was with Jesus. He healed people of their physical illnesses, but there were times when he discerned that they needed inner healing also. He was concerned about healing the whole person – the physical, spiritual and emotional. This is what we see in the incident of the woman who touched the edge of his cloak.

Mark describes the woman in 5:25–6. She had been ill for twelve years. Subject to bleeding. An embarrassing illness, which even today we might refer to as 'woman's trouble'. She had suffered a great deal under the care of many doctors and had spent all her money. But instead of getting better, she had got worse.

Imagine how you would feel if you spent all your savings on a private operation because there was such a long waiting list on the NHS, but at the end of it you were actually worse rather than better. You would feel devastated.

But what made her suffering even worse was the fact that, in her society, her illness made her ceremonially unclean, and anyone who touched her was deemed to be unclean. Not only that, but anything she touched became unclean, and if someone then touched that item they also became unclean and had to go through a purification ritual. All this would have affected her relationships with family and friends. If she was married, it would have put an end to the physical relationship with her husband. No hugs and kisses from her children. She could not go out in public, she could not mix with people socially, she could not attend the synagogue or temple; she became an outcast.

Physical healing

The woman had heard of Jesus and his power to heal, but when he came to her village she had a problem. She was not supposed to be near people in case she touched them and made them unclean. She was certainly not supposed to touch a Rabbi. If she came openly, there would be an outcry against her in that small community where everyone knew everyone. However, a large crowd had gathered around Jesus, probably including a lot of strangers, so she decided to risk creeping in among the crowd and secretly touching the edge of Jesus' cloak. Surely that would not do any harm? Surely she could creep away again, and nobody but her would know what she had done?

All went well at first. She saw her chance when Jesus stopped to speak to Jairus. While the attention of the crowd was on the two men, she came up behind Jesus, reached out and touched his cloak and was immediately healed. But then she turned to get away and found that it wasn't so easy. The crowd was pressing in and there was no escape. What was worse, Jesus turned round in the crowd and asked: 'Who touched my clothes?' (Mark 5:30, NIV). The disciples thought it was a daft question. 'The people are crowding against you. How can you ask: "Who touched my clothes?" Lots of people are touching your clothes.' But Jesus knew that this was no ordinary touch. It was the touch of faith, and healing power had gone out from him. So he kept looking around to see who had done it. The woman was afraid. She had been found out. This was not part of the plan. Surely Jesus would be angry with her for touching him and making him unclean.

Why didn't Jesus just let the woman go? He knew she had been physically healed. Why did he want to cause her such embarrassment by singling her out in public? Yes, Jesus knew the woman had been healed physically. But he discerned that this was someone who needed deeper healing – healing of the spirit and the emotions.

Eventually, the woman comes forward trembling with fear. Expecting a rebuke, she falls down before him, confessing what she has done as if it were a crime, expecting his anger. To her amazement, and no doubt to the amazement of the crowd, rather than being angry with her, Jesus commends her and says: 'Daughter, your faith has healed you. Go in peace and be freed from your suffering' (v. 34, NIV).

The woman has already been healed physically, but Jesus now wants to bring the woman inner healing because, in addition to her physical suffering, there was the spiritual and emotional suffering of isolation.

Spiritual healing

The woman's illness not only debarred her from society, it also debarred her from the synagogue and the temple because her bleeding made her ritually unclean. In those days, people thought it was necessary to go to the synagogue or the temple to pray and to worship. It was not normal to pray and worship at home. Nor could she read God's word. Women did not learn to read. People did not have a Bible in their home. The scrolls were kept in the synagogue. So, even if she could read, which was unlikely, she could not get access to them. This meant that she had no means of fellowship with God.

Jesus first of all makes it clear that there is no magic in his clothes. Lots of people were touching him that day. But it is her faith that has healed her. God heard her prayer even in her unclean state. She was acceptable to him even before she was physically healed. Jesus calls her 'Daughter', indicating that she is accepted and loved as a member of the family of God. He sets her free from her spiritual isolation, sets her free to belong.

Emotional healing

But further healing is still needed. For twelve years, she has been carrying an inner pain because of her sense of emotional isolation. Now this will be compounded because she has a guilty secret. She should not have been out in the crowd. She should not have touched Jesus. So, how would she explain her sudden healing to her family and neighbours?

Perhaps you have an inner pain or a guilty secret. It may be something that you did in the past, it may be some hurt that has been done to you, it may be something that is happening right now. In order to be set free from the inner suffering, that secret must be brought to the surface. It can be a very painful process and usually needs the help of someone who can be trusted. It takes courage to come forward. But, until that secret is confronted and dealt with, you will never be free; you will never be completely healed.

The woman's illness was public knowledge in that little village, and so Jesus asks her to come forward and explain what has happened so that she might be publicly healed and set free. Jesus makes it clear that he has not been defiled by the woman. Rather, he has made her clean. She is acceptable to him. The woman has been a social outcast for twelve years. Everyone in the village knows about her illness. Jesus makes this public declaration so that she will be accepted back into society again. She is therefore to go in peace and be freed from her suffering. No need to keep that guilty secret. Jesus sets her free from her emotional isolation, sets her free to belong.

Illustration

Jesus came to bring people complete healing – physical, spiritual and emotional. Sometimes a physical illness can be a means of finding inner healing. This happened to me some years ago when I had chronic fatigue then cancer. My illness set me on a new path where, through the help of loving counsellors, I found healing for spiritual and emotional hurts of the past. These inner wounds were contributing to my illness, and so it was important that I found spiritual and emotional healing as well as physical healing.

Conclusion

Jesus came to bring people complete healing. We tend to look only for physical healing, just as the woman who touched his cloak did. But Jesus sees below the surface to your deeper needs, and wants to bring you emotional and spiritual healing, which is even more important than physical healing.

He wants to say to you: 'My daughter, my son, your faith has healed you. Go in peace and be freed from your suffering.'

The Wise Woman
in My Soul

REV. JENNY WILLIAMS

I wrote 'Wise Woman' for this book. Study of the Wisdom tradition has significantly helped my understanding of Jesus, the Word and Wisdom of God. The healing aspect of Jesus' ministry is threaded through with wisdom, a deep understanding of life, passionate, wild, nurturing, mysterious and loving. And in which culture are these characteristics not recognised as feminine?

You were there at my birth but I did not see you
    I saw a family in which men were valued
    It was not clear what women were ...
    I only knew that I did not seem to belong
You were there, silent, for I could not yet hear and understand
    And I was silent, too, not able to voice my pain, my
        shame,
    wanting not to be a woman, not to be silenced,
        controlled, reduced
    my nameless self hidden, watching
    only knowing what I did want

You joined with me in my adamant stand
You spoke into my heart words of reassurance that things could
    be different
You gave birth to hope in me

The Wise Woman in My Soul

I did not know your name
> I made brave efforts to be as good as men
> Studied hard, did the right things and pretended I was
> > not woman

You gave me men outside the family who recognised my call
Who showed me that I had potential to minister
> Stunned I said 'no'

You were very quiet, giving me space and time to grow
> to know more of myself

Jesus – whom I knew as lover
Who sustained me and gave my life meaning and direction
Jesus – whom I rejected for a while
So masculine and different from me
Seemingly not meeting me in my illness
My confusion creating clouds of despair

I could feel you – but found no shape or form that fitted
Years of knowing and not knowing
Years of not knowing and knowing

Waters of my heart breaking

Very stealthily and quietly you have revealed more of yourself
Word made flesh, Wisdom of God,
Breathing into me stillness,
A mirror where I see
You … the Wise Woman in my Soul

The Good Partner

REV. CAROL FORD

This reflection was welcomed by my Church of Scotland congregation because civil partnerships were being discussed at that time in Presbyteries, in Life & Work and in Ministers' Forum. There were also members of the congregation trying to decide whether or not ministers could use their pastoral conscience to bless such relationships if they felt it appropriate. Several people engaged in conversation with me at this time. The reflection opened doors of debate, exploration and a closer look at Scriptural references. It is a continuing journey, but openness has been encouraged.

Jesus said: 'My command is this: Love each other as I have loved you' (John 15:12, NIV).

'Marriage is a gift of God based on His loving nature,
    and is His promise of love with us in Christ.
Husband and wife, in giving themselves to each other,
    reflect the love of Christ
    in a complete loving relationship
    through times of happiness and times of challenge.'
'Marriage is a way of life,
    to be honoured and to be worked at,
    and invites a life-long commitment to each other's good
    in a union of strength, sensitivity and trust.'

These are statements that I use in every wedding in St Margaret's.

This week, I had the privilege of visiting and eating with a couple who have been married for many years. It is a truly blessed relationship, and they are mutually good partners. In their company, you are enfolded in the love and joy they still find in each other and in the world God has gifted them. Even if you arrive feeling very upbeat, you still leave feeling somehow better and more wholesome. The Church upholds the sanctity of marriage. A genuine loving relationship images God.

Our Proverbs reading (31:10–31) is entitled in some translations 'The Virtuous Woman' and in others 'The Capable Wife'. There are many listed duties of the wife that are relevant only to the status of women in Old Testament times, when a woman was little more than a husband's property. Today, women have very different roles in society and a much greater freedom of choice. But there are characteristics of the woman in this Bible reading that are appropriate to describing any good partner.

She is more valuable than the most precious gem. Her husband trusts her. He is enriched and made more by her love. She is a creative force in his life who does him good. She never undermines him or is a destructive influence on his life. All these qualities should be mutual in a good partnership. The woman also gives to the needy and is a good mother. She is wise and kind. She is respected in her community. She honours God.

The attributes – not all the precise roles she performs – the attributes of this wife in her love of God, partner, family and neighbour are good benchmarks not only of family values in the historical context but also for today in terms of love and faithfulness.

God is our Maker. God is always faithful and loving. God is a force of good in our lives. God wants the best for each of us. God is the perfect partner.

Civil partnerships became legal in Scotland in December 2005. The law does not make provision for any religious element in a civil-partnership ceremony. Naturally, those in same-sex partnerships who are committed Christians are asking ministers if they can receive a blessing on their relationship. Some ministers have agreed to the request, while others have refused because they believe it would be wrong for them to do so. I believe that freedom of pastoral conscience is crucial in allowing a minister to exercise his or her ministry according to the leading of the Holy Spirit, interpretation of Scripture and personal knowledge of the relational circumstances of those to whom we minister.

I must tell you that I would bless a same-sex relationship that I knew to be long-standing, faithful and loving. Here is why.

When Moses asked God's name, God said: **'I am who I am'** (Exodus 3:14, NIV). God can be no other. This is God's nature. **'I am who I am.'** The Bible teaches us that we **'are made in the image of God'**. Believing that to be so, we can say not only **'I am whose I am'** but also **'I am who I am'**.

It is a vital part of our very humanity to be able to say: **'Lord, I am the person whom You created and are still creating me to be'**. To be faithful, *we* can be no other.

But someone who has grown up knowing from childhood or early teen years that he or she is a homosexual cannot say **'I am who I am'** without risk, even in the Church which purports to be a corporate body of love. For many God-loving, committed Christian homosexuals, **'I am who I am'** can only be prayed and whispered in private. In the Church and outside, they can only say 'I am who you will allow me to be'.

An integral part of who we are is whom we love and who loves us. God lives in relationship, Father, Son and Holy Spirit. Genuine loving relationships image God.

'Love God and love one another as I have loved you.' That is Jesus' core teaching!

LIVE IN LOVE.

Jesus was inclusive. He stood beside everyone who came to him. He knew their stories. He knew when folk lived in true love and when they didn't. He saw right through the Samaritan woman at the well with her many husbands and present partner. He saw through the hypocrites who flung the woman caught in adultery at Jesus' feet. He did not condemn the woman. He said: 'Go and sin no more', meaning: 'Go and live in a monogamous faithful relationship with someone you really love'.

Jesus would identify with the suffering of growing up as a homosexual in society where heterosexuality will always be the norm. Jesus knew how hard it was to be different and not fit in with the expectations of the world. Jesus supported the excluded and the underdogs. Jesus hears the cry of the young man or woman who falls on their knees and cries: '**God, why did you make me like this? Please help me, I am so lonely.**'

Jesus sees the tears of the homosexual who wants to love God and a same-sex friend but fears rejection and alienation from family and church, unless he or she remains hidden. Let us remember that homosexuality is about family values. Whatever happens to us happens to the people who love us. Many a family has journeyed to hell and back trying to understand a son or a daughter, a sister or a brother trying to come to terms with their sexual orientation. The Church needs to be a listening and healing place for these families. Are we?

The Bible does not give us unequivocal guidance. Old Testament references are to specific homosexual acts that are linked to orgies and breach of hospitality. They have nothing to do with love. There is no teaching about monogamous, loving homosexual relationships.

The Church is an inclusive family of which Christ is the head. We breach his hospitality if we do not welcome all who love the Lord. If the Church marks civil partnerships where each looks to the good of the other in mutual love, trust and faithfulness, we are blessing a relationship that images God. And we are affirming the humanity of each person in that partnership. We are saying: 'It's OK, you can be a Christian and say with your life: "I am who I am"'.

Blessing and grace come from God. Grace is not ours to keep. It is God's unconditional love. God will bless who and what God chooses. We will not control God. But, as the body of Christ on earth, who and what we bless is done in Jesus' name. And I believe that Jesus would look into the hearts of people as He always has done, and bless those who love each other as Jesus himself loves us. At the end of the day, God will be the judge of that – and surely that judgement will be: '**How well did you love in My name**?' Amen.

Acting on Impulse

REV. ROSIE FREW

A colleague and I were reminiscing recently about recording *Thought for the Day* for Radio Tay, many years ago now. We had to go to the studios on a Sunday afternoon and record five 'Thoughts' for the following week. Each 'Thought' had to last 55 seconds – no more, no less.

I remember spending hours preparing these scripts. I wanted to say something meaningful, something appropriate, something memorable, something light-hearted and something serious – all in 55 seconds! It was not easy.

The 'Thought' I still remember was entitled 'Acting on Impulse' – though, given the strictures of recording, there was not much room for impulsiveness there. I took my inspiration from a television advert for a perfumed body spray and my disillusionment that, despite wearing it, I had still not received one bunch of flowers from an admirer who just couldn't help 'acting on impulse'!

I related that to the story of Mary of Bethany, who anointed Jesus with expensive perfume – a woman who acted impulsively and extravagantly, much to the annoyance of the disciples (Matthew 26:6–13). Yet, had she not acted when she did, on impulse, she would have missed the opportunity forever.

William Barclay wrote of her action:

> It shows us that certain things must be done when the opportunity arises, or they can never be done at all. ...

There are some things which we can do at any time; there are some things which can be done only once; and to miss the opportunity to do them then is to miss the opportunity forever. Often we are moved by some generous impulse, and do not act upon it; and all the chances are that the circumstances, the person, the time and the impulse will never return. For so many of us, the tragedy is that life is the history of the lost opportunities to do the lovely thing. (*The New Daily Study Bible: The Gospel of Matthew*, vol. 2 (Edinburgh: Saint Andrew Press, 2001), p. 386)

We all have our regrets; we've all had cause to say 'if only' ... So, when that person or that thought comes into your mind, it could be God giving you a nudge – go on, act on impulse, don't miss the opportunity. Make the phone call, send the card, buy the flowers, give the donation, pay the visit ...

Standing on Holy Ground

REV. JEAN MONTGOMERIE

I feel that this refocuses minds on the central reason we gather together – to worship Almighty God. Taking off your shoes fairly instils the message. I hope that this piece will give someone a springboard to develop his or her own worship service. A germ of an idea is often all it takes.

READINGS: Exodus 3:1–6 and Matthew 18:15–20

Part 1

'Standing on holy ground'

Consider your reaction if, each time you came to worship, you were asked to remove your shoes. Yes, of course, we've all been to places where it has been *de rigueur* to cover our heads when entering a place of worship while we've been on holiday – and some may even have had the experience of removing their footwear while visiting the holy places of Islam, or of the Indian subcontinent. Consider, then, God's command to Moses as he approaches the Burning Bush. 'Take off your sandals.' Now, Moses' sandals protected him not only from the stony ground of the desert but also, to a lesser degree, from scorpions and snakes. So, this was no casual request that God made. Moses was being asked to make himself vulnerable, to leave the contamination of his daily life behind, because the place of meeting with God was holy ground.

Friends, this building was once dedicated to the glory of God, and for the sole purpose of providing a meeting place where folk could come to worship, and where we might expect Christ's promise to be fulfilled that where two or three are gathered together in his name, he is here among us. It therefore follows that we should treat this place, at this hour, as holy ground, and consider what sandals God asks us to discard in his presence. They might be the sandals of self-assurance – the shell we have grown which allows no other access to our innermost thoughts. On the other hand, they might be the sandals of doubt – breeding a lack of expectation that God can work a work for you today. They may be the sandals of guilt, or of longing, of disillusionment, or of helplessness. Whatever your sandals and mine, God invites us to take them off now, for we stand on holy ground.

At this point, invite folk who are comfortable with the exercise to remove their shoes and, sitting or standing, to sing 'Be still, for the presence of the Lord ...'.

Part 2

Holy relationships

Whether you are now sitting with your actual shoes off, or whether we have simply given thought to the sandals that God has invited us to remove so that we are open to his presence, the reading from Matthew's Gospel is a word from the Lord. For, while we prefer to imagine that disagreements and hurts belong to the world outside the church, here, stripped of our pretensions, we are asked to confront the fact that broken relationships do occur from time to time – even in the Church family, but further, that it is unthinkable in the Christian community that these situations should remain unresolved.

As many of you know, one of my childhood heroes was Corrie ten Boom, a woman who lived out and struggled with her faith through internment in concentration camps during the Second World War, and for many years after the war as she travelled the world, sharing her experience and her faith. Listen to one of her struggles with this issue:

[Read from *Tramp for the Lord*, pp. 180–2.]

So, let's take a moment in contemplation to identify those broken relationships in our Church community and in our private lives, seeking God's help to heal our attitudes of the past.

Plan Be

REV. MARY HADDOW

'Plan Be' is the basis for sermons. I thought it might be useful as either reflections or starting points for a sermon. The material worked well within my congregation because it built on previous themes.

We have all heard of 'Plan A'. Here is 'PLAN BE'.

We all have people in our lives who seem to have had a 'joy bypass': those who seem to be fault-finding; who chant the words 'it's aye been this way' or 'we tried that before and it didn't work'; those who want to suck the joy out of your life. And we are called to love them. The thing is, we need to guard our hearts against them too, because sometimes they want to drag us down into the basement of life where they feel we should reside, thus showing their power.

All of us have the potential to be 'basement people' for others, yet we are called to BE ENCOURAGING. Encouragement is the language of the New Testament:

1 Thessalonians 5:11 (NIV)

Therefore, encourage one another and build each other up ...

Hebrews 3:13 (NIV)

But encourage one another daily, as long as it is called Today, so that none of you may be hardened by sin's deceitfulness ...

Hebrews 10:25 (NIV)

> Let us not give up meeting together as some are in the habit of doing, but let us encourage one another.

The exhortation 'to encourage' is used countless times in the New Testament, probably because one of the great things about encouragement is that it always spirals up, never down.

So, whom can you encourage today? Whom can you lift out of the basement of life?

Plan Be: Be with

A great community is where it is safe to be the real you. As you sit in church or in a Bible Study, look around. These are the people you are called into community with. Do you know them? Do you know the joys and the sorrows that they are facing at this point in their lives? Are you willing to come alongside and help? Are you willing to be real with each other? To pray for each other?

1 Peter 3:8–9 (NIV) tells us:

> live in harmony with one another; be sympathetic, love as brothers, be compassionate and humble. Do not repay evil with evil or insult with insult, but with blessing . . .

Jesus says in Matthew 18:20 (NIV):

> For where two or three come together in my name, there am I.

> You come together in my name and devote yourselves to each other, and I'll be right there with you. Support one another, pray for one another, don't try to undermine someone just because you don't get your own way. When someone gets it wrong, don't try to belittle them. Remember you are my community, and I am right here with you. Listening. Watching. Still trying to teach you.

That's Jesus' 'Be With' plan. Are you part of his plan?

Plan Be: Be extravagant

Many of you will recall the film *Zorba the Greek*. There is some advice given to the hero, the sentiments of which I think many would benefit from remembering. The hero was seated on an old, wise man's knee. The wise old man told him that God was so immense, he could never be contained by heaven or by earth. But there was one place in which he could be, and that was within the human heart. The young lad was advised never to wound another person's heart.

Jesus is on his way to the cross. It's just a few days before Passover. The chief priests and scribes are plotting against him. Judas is about ready to betray him. The crucifixion is less than a week away, and Jesus knows it.

Jesus and his disciples stop at Bethany. Just a few days before, Jesus had raised Lazarus from the dead there in Bethany. Now, as they are having dinner, a woman comes to Jesus and does a beautiful but extravagant thing for our Lord. She brings an alabaster jar of very expensive ointment; she breaks open the jar and pours the costly perfumed oil on Jesus' feet (John 12:1–8). She anoints him with oil. One thing is clear: whatever meanings scholars may attach to Mary's act of anointing Jesus with precious oil, it was without question an act of love and kindness; an act of extravagant generosity and graciousness. Now, on the Thursday night of that week, there was a meal with friends ... there was an act of betrayal ... an arrest ... desertion by friends ...

Can you imagine how that must have wounded his heart?

There were six trials that night – and, during one trial, Jesus was brought before Pilate, the Roman governor. We're told:

'Now it was the governor's custom at the Feast to release a prisoner chosen by the crowd' (Matthew 27:15ff., NIV).

The crowd that was present was given a choice: they could choose Jesus, the man of grace and peace, or Barabbas, the man of intolerance and violence. These two men offered two different kinds of revolution. Jesus offered a new quality of life and a new way of living. The people had heard Jesus teach and seen him heal. Barabbas offered the way of armed rebellion against the Roman Empire. The people knew he had been imprisoned for murder. The crowd made their choice. They chose freedom for the man of intolerance and violence, and a violent death for the man of grace and peace.

Can you imagine how that must have wounded his heart? And now we have to ask the question: which is more successful? The way of intolerance and violence, or the way of grace and peace?

When we think of intolerance and violence, what do we think of? This week, on Monday 26 March 2007, there was so much violence reported in our world. On that one date, seventy-two were killed in bombings in Iraq and eighty-two were injured. In the capital of Congo, sixty died and seventy-four were injured. Reports came in about murders, attacks, abuse.

On Monday, there was also an historic event going on. Its headline read: 'An historic day for peace ...'. And, from around the world, people sent words of encouragement and praised the extraordinary act of reconciliation between the Unionist and Republican leaders of Northern Ireland.

They have tried the way of intolerance and violence; now they are trying the way of peace.

The thing to remember is that we always have a choice. Mary chose the way of extravagant generosity and graciousness. Judas, the religious leaders, and the crowd, chose the way of intolerance and violence.

In this past week, we may have been in conflict with someone and shown intolerance and violence in our words and actions. In doing so, what we have shown is ugly – an unattractiveness that in no way reflects Christ's grace and peace.

Sometime this week, perhaps today, we might get into an argument with someone. As we get more and more angry, we might be tempted to hit out, and believe me we all do it more than perhaps we're aware, because hitting out can be with words as much as with fists. But, before it gets too heated, we still have a choice.

Which will we choose? The way of intolerance and violence, or the way of grace and peace?

The point is: will we act with grace in order to build peace? Or will there be such a lack of grace in our dealings with others that we no longer show the face of Christ to those around us, as we strike out and wound another person's heart? In words and actions, Jesus taught us that we're supposed to be extravagant in our generosity and graciousness towards others. Mary followed that example while others chose another way.

The spirit of Christ can empower and enable us to be extravagant in our generosity and to be extravagant in our graciousness, but the choice is still ours. We write our own headlines.

So, what would your personal headline for last week have read like? Would it have spoken of your generosity and grace?

The Power of Words

REV. ANNE ATTENBURROW

This reflection was delivered at a Healing Service at the culmination of a weekend of Meditation and Healing. I think it spoke to people's hearts. Many people came forward for healing.

> Surely he hath borne our griefs, and carried our sorrows: yet we did esteem him stricken, smitten of God, and afflicted. But he was wounded for our transgressions, he was bruised for our iniquities: the chastisement of our peace was upon him, and with his stripes we are healed. All we like sheep have gone astray, we have turned every one to his own way; and the LORD hath laid on him the iniquity of us all. (Isaiah 53:4–6, AV)

The theme of this short reflection is THE POWER OF WORDS – in particular, the power of the words we have in this book, the Bible; the Word of God. We will focus on one particular phrase central to our text from Isaiah 53, and central to our Gospel message:

> 'With his stripes we are healed'.

However, initially, I'd like to tell you a story about a man living in the mid-eighteenth century. He had come upon hard times, he was up to his eyes in debt and he was in serious risk of being confined in the debtor's prison. He was deeply depressed, he had lost all his energy and vigour, he could not sleep and he was plagued with rheumatism. He probably thought: 'Is life really worth living?' That man was George Frederick Handel, the famous composer.

In the midst of these dark and desolate times, two letters fell on his doormat. One was from the Duke of Devonshire inviting him to Dublin to produce a series of benefit concerts for the relief of prisoners, the sick and the poor. The other one was from a wealthy but eccentric English landowner, Charles Jennens; in that letter was a compilation of Old and New Testament passages outlining the Gospel story.

Handel read those words again and again. He was greatly moved and re-energised. He wrote an oratorio based on those words, a kind of spiritual opera, which I think we all know well: the *Messiah*. The miracle is that from his hapless and miserable state, after reading those words, he wrote the whole oratorio in just three weeks. Those words from the Scriptures seemed to have awakened him from his lethargy. They had been healing in some way.

The oratorio, the *Messiah*, was and still is a tremendous success. Handel's fortunes were restored; but not only that, the income from the performances fed the hungry, cared for prisoners and clothed the naked: Christ's calling and thus our calling. Those powerful words of Scripture, outlining the Gospel story, turned Handel's life around and many others. Central to the oratorio is the chorus singing the words:

> Surely, He hath borne our griefs, and carried our sorrows. He was wounded for our transgressions, He was bruised for our iniquities. The chastisement of our peace was upon Him. And with His stripes we are healed.

Did these words hit home to Handel, I wonder? Did the reality of these words transform him and heal him?

'With his stripes we are healed.'

Do we truly acknowledge the reality and the power of these words?

Firstly, do we really, truly acknowledge the healing power of God? After all, God did say: '*I, the Lord, am your healer*' right back in Moses' time. This isn't a new, trendy idea. God has always had the power to heal in whatever way he thinks fit.

Secondly, do we really acknowledge the cost of that healing? We were all shocked and disgusted by the graphic portrayal of Jesus' flagellation and crucifixion in the film *The Passion of the Christ*. I know I closed my eyes at each blow; I could not bear to look. Many people said that such violence should not be shown – but isn't that because, in our minds and our hearts, we have sanitised the humiliation, the torture and the crucifixion of Jesus? We can't bear it because it was our sins that ripped, crushed and tore at him. OUR SINS! We think that, as he was the Son of God, Jesus somehow rose above the pain and humiliation; but he was crucified as a human being on our behalf: he felt it all! Jesus did it for us, for our healing; healing of our relationship with God and healing of our minds, our bodies and our souls. He did it at such cost!

Such knowledge, such powerful words should bring us to tears – grateful tears! Tears of joy for all that our Lord has done for us. For 'With his stripes we are *indeed* healed'.

Consider the Lilies

REV. JOAN CRAIG

I hope that this meditation will remind readers of the other side of the idyllic pastoral scene: the fraught, risky business of producing food. I hope, too, that it will encourage others to wrestle similarly with thunderclouds, rain and rainbows in the business of giving thanks in their diverse circumstances.

Harvest thanksgiving! What are we to give thanks for? Wet barley? Blasted oats? The high cost of fuel and inputs and the low returns? The rip-off prices of the supermarket overlords? The ongoing trading problems abroad?

Name your gripes, your frustration, your resentment, your despair. Name them. You can't give thanks for these compounded difficulties, which are so beyond your control, which so seek to thwart your hard endeavours. But you can name them. You must name them and not hoard them up inside. If you do, they'll fester and moulder like barley without popcorn and bring all the more disaster. So name them. Give thanks that you *can* name them. If you can do that, you can share them with others. In the sharing, put them into perspective, reduce them to size, savour the support of understanding neighbours and friends. They won't be able to magic away the problems, but they can stand shoulder to shoulder in solidarity. Thus you can stand the slings and arrows of outrageous misfortune.

Then lift your eyes again to the hills and give thanks:

Give thanks for the chance
> to idle along the road in the tractor
> to lift your eyes to the hills of Hoy and Wideford
> to look on the sunrise glistening on black Copinsay
> to savour the setting sun over the silky blue sea
> to rest your gaze on the reflections in St Peter's Pool

Give thanks for the hope
> of the sign of the rainbow
> of the magic of new birth
> of tidy furrows ploughed, and the thought
> of the green shoots rising another year.

Give thanks for generations past who remained faithful in harsher times than ours, who have given us the gifts of this place, of our own life, our own skills, our own faith.

Give thanks that there is increasing appreciation of the work on the land, that there is a meeting of minds and concern between farmers and consumers, at farm gate and farmers' markets.

Give thanks that there is a growing realisation that trade must be fair.

Give thanks for fellow farmers the world over who, with more grief than ours, produce the bounty for us of coffee and chocolate, of cotton and coconut, of spices and nuts and delectable fruits.

Give thanks for the supper on the table, bread on the board: work of human hands, gift of God.

Give thanks to God for his bounty of wisdom and strength that endures, and which enables us to endure.

Consider the lilies of the field, the primroses and flags, and appreciate God's provision. What is truly needed will be given. What is truly needed is relatively little. Like the lilies, we are part of a vast created order that is sustained by the Creator. Our part in that order is to consider the lilies – to be considerate of them, to ensure that their beauty and ours continues. We do well to give thanks for the privilege.

A Fragile Peace

REV. GILLEAN MACLEAN

I wrote this poem for the conclusion of an early-morning service.

A fragile peace rests on my heart
as the fluttering of the day begins.
I reach beyond,
for silence.
A deep warming quietness
that closes round me like a velvet glove
that travels with me through all.
The peace of God
that never passes
but remains.
And I go forward
quietly trusting
that
God is Good.

A Cord that Must be Broken

REV. PAULINE STEENBERGEN

*This poem was written from the personal experience of leaving con-
gregations and how painful this can be for a minister. It was written
after the birth of my son following a very rough labour and delivery.
It struck me that letting go of a charge could be like what a surrogate
mum must feel – handing on a precious life to someone else to take care
of and nurture. This poem seems to appeal to colleagues and friends
who have been in their last weeks of a ministry and have so many mixed
emotions.*

Lord,
Soon I am required to break this pastoral tie.

I picture my people …

I have carried them inside me:
in my head, heart, body.
I have carried their worries and sadnesses,
their hurts and pain and losses;
their joys and healing.
Together, Lord, we have fed them faithfully,
Sunday by Sunday (day by day).
Nurtured them by prayer and action.
Loved them even when that loving was sore and hard
(and they have loved me back).
They have grown.
I have grown.

Sometimes it just feels too soon.
How can it be time to let go?

Did you feel all this too, Lord Jesus?
Did you struggle and wrestle with your Father when the time
came?

(Was your stomach churning,
so full of emotion at the Last Supper?
Was it hard to eat?)

As my hour approaches,
lend me the help that you yourself found.
Soon, Lord, too soon I am required to break this pastoral tie.
Perhaps only then will I realise that this will bring new life for
both of us.
New joy, new hope, new love – a new future.

Here, Lord, I picture my people and place them in your hands.

They belong to you.

Cut the cord gently.

Wrap
them
in
your

Love ...

Section 5
Biblical Characters

Martha

REV. LINDSAY SCHLUTER

I have never wondered why, of the two sisters, Mary is the one that men in the Church find the more attractive. After all, she sits adoringly at a man's feet, never says a word and, when required, suitably dissolves into tears. We have no idea of what she thinks or what her faith is. But I have always wondered why so many women have bought into the notion that Martha is secondary to Mary, that she is supposedly too much of a housewife to be concerned with the things of faith. There is only a tiny handful of people in the Gospel accounts who openly confess their faith in Jesus as the Messiah. Martha is one of them. She knows her theology, she articulates it clearly. And then she makes the bold statement that she shares with Peter and the centurion at the cross. Martha, to me, is a supremely important role model for women in the Church – and my idea to give her a beautiful earring in this poem is done in the hope of showing that there is far more to her than pots and pans and restless activity.

Deep in her pocket she finds it.
The earring she had thought lost.
    Silver, with precious stones.
       Bold.
          Beautifully crafted.
Now it is all entangled after days in her pocket.
    Carefully she lifts it,
       Disentangles it.

Places it on the table in front of her.
She had worn the earrings for him.
On that day, yearning for something.
He had found it, the earring,
on that day when she had gone out to meet him.
The day she had found him, had found herself.
Her brother had died.
Her friend had not come.
He had not come in time.
She had worn the earrings for him.
Silver framing her face.
And he had been too late.
Too late even for her, the sensible one.
When he did come, she went out to meet him.
And he met her,
Took her, only her,
with him to a new place.
Earrings, a brother dead,
they were not in this place.
Only two people.
And in that place he met her:
in her yearning
in her fragility.
Martha the strong one.

He met her,
gave her new life,
a new beginning.
Do you believe?
Yes, I believe.

Deep in her pocket she finds it.
The earring he had found, caught in her dress that day.
He had given it back to her,
placed gently in the palm of his hand.

And she had returned to the place
she had come from:
     A sister, the visitors …
That earring –
she will wear it now.
Will wear it for him, the son of God,
     who had come to meet her.
          Her alone.

Doubting Mary and the Camomile Tissues

REV. YVONNE HENDRIE

Based on the story of Doubting Thomas, this piece grew from my experiences of being a hospice chaplain. This role challenged and informed my faith. Several people felt encouraged by this sermon to speak to me afterwards about similar experiences to the one I had had regarding the scent of camomile.

Reading: John 20:24–31

Not long after I became a hospice chaplain, I met a lovely lady called Mary. Mary was 60 and was about to celebrate her ruby wedding anniversary. Mary also had cancer and had only a few months to live.

The first thing I did after introducing myself to Mary was sneeze, because I was suffering from the sniffles; and Mary, being the lovely soul she was, was more concerned about my health than her own. She reached over to her bedside cabinet and lifted a box of camomile-scented tissues, telling me how soothing they were, and pulling out enough of them to fill my pockets.

We began to chat; and, as chaplains tend to do, I let Mary lead the conversation.

That first visit was confined to small talk, which is often the case until people, especially vulnerable people, get to know you. On the second visit, however, Mary became tearful and said there was something troubling her. She seemed to think she was the only one who had ever asked me this question, but I reassured her that some people in her situation do question their faith.

Mary was wondering if her soul really would live on. She found herself worrying about whether or not there was a Heaven, or was she facing oblivion? And if there was a Heaven, was she going there? She began confessing regrets about a few things in her life – and believe me, they were paltry compared to some of the confessions I've heard. Well, over the course of that visit and the ones that followed, Mary and I studied what the Scriptures have to say about the afterlife, and we discussed what it might be like, because to be truthful, nobody this side of eternity really knows. As we talked about these things, Mary was in her bed and I was on a chair by the bed, and the scent from her box of camomile tissues wafted around us in the warm hospice atmosphere.

One day, after several visits, Mary said: 'Yes, I think I do believe that I'll live on after this life; and if I do, I'll come back and let you know'. Now, Mary was perfectly serious about this. She thought that if she could just get a message to me after she had died, then I could use that to comfort others. I told her that I was certain in any case – that, because of the promises of Jesus, I didn't require any proof.

Well, the inevitable happened, and, after a while, during which our friendship blossomed, Mary died peacefully. Speaking professionally and pastorally, it had been a very satisfying relationship. I felt that this lady, who had been ashamed to admit her doubts, had been helped – because she discovered that it's okay to have doubts; and it's the right thing to do, to ask questions; and God will not judge us for our honesty.

Three days after Mary died, I woke up very suddenly in the early hours of a March morning. There was a gentle breeze blowing in the room, and I couldn't understand it, because no windows were open. There was also a scent wafting on the breeze, and, as I lay there puzzling about what it was, it grew stronger.

I realised that it was the scent of camomile. I also realised that I had absolutely nothing scented with camomile in the house. Then I remembered Mary, and her tissues; and suddenly the breeze and the perfume disappeared. Was I really asleep and dreaming? I'm sure I wasn't.

Was my mind playing a trick on me? I don't know. How far can we trust our senses?

As far as Doubting Thomas was concerned, only the sense of touch could really be trusted. The other disciples all claimed to have seen Jesus risen from the dead, but that wasn't enough for Thomas. He wasn't going to believe unless he could actually touch his wounds.

We tend to be rather hard on Thomas. Fancy doubting when all the other disciples told him what they had seen with their own eyes! Those of us with health and strength might think the same about Mary – fancy doubting there's a Heaven! It's easy to judge when we're not in somebody else's shoes, isn't it? There was Mary, afraid and struggling towards the end – and there was Thomas, who'd lost his leader and his friend, who was grief-stricken, depressed and defeated, saying: 'Nah, you've got it wrong'.

Have we tried to imagine the scene, though? There are all the other disciples, ecstatic and filled with joy; and Thomas must have wanted to believe them, he didn't want his friend to be dead. The easiest thing to do would have been to join in with the celebrations, even if he thought they were all crazy. Go along with it, play the same game, pretend for a while that this terrible thing hasn't happened. It actually took courage to admit his doubts. Think about any time you've been in a group who are all saying one thing. Even if you disagree strongly, it's hard to come out and say it, isn't it? I think it's high time Thomas was given some credit for his courage and his honesty. And I think it's high time there was more of it in Christian circles.

I had the utmost respect for the Church of England priest whose daughter was killed in the London bombings of July 2005, and who had the courage and honesty to admit that she could not forgive the terrorist. On grounds of conscience, she resigned from the priesthood. It would have been so much easier to put on a pious countenance and keep her job. How can any of us really know how we would react in the situations that others found themselves in?

Courage and honesty. Those qualities made Thomas able to have his doubts answered quickly. Jesus appeared in the flesh and invited him to do what he needed to do in order to believe. For those of us who have followed in the long years since Christ ascended into Heaven, it isn't as simple as that.

'Blessed are those who have not seen, and yet come to believe', said Jesus (John 20:29, NRSV). But Thomas still stands for us as the example of the fact that it's better to doubt and to admit it than to pretend. I've worked with patients who did both. There were those who delighted in putting on a pious countenance for the chaplain, telling me all the reasons why their place in Heaven was assured, indeed how they were looking forward to getting there. It didn't always ring true. Often, I felt that those who admitted they were struggling and afraid had more integrity. Not that the others were to be judged; but they simply couldn't admit how fearful they really were, because they had been conditioned into saying 'the right thing', the acceptable thing which they thought would impress the chaplain.

Throughout the Bible, there are people who express their doubts about various aspects of faith and belief; and their stories are there because they matter, because they were real people with real concerns. We, too, are real people with real concerns. We may have doubts from time to time; perhaps some niggle away a lot of the time. Perhaps we think we're the only one who thinks this way; that others will judge us if we admit it; and so, we take the easy route, smile and show nothing, ask no questions in case it makes us look bad.

What we forget is that faith is a journey rather than a destination. We don't suddenly arrive at 'Perfect Faith'. We stumble along the way; sometimes we take one step forwards and two back; there are obstacles in our path. As we journey in faith, we have to be honest and ask questions. Wouldn't God prefer us to be honest seekers, rather than pious pretenders?

Colourful Characters

REV. SARAH ROSS

The colour theme was used to help people understand the different colours of the liturgical year and to encourage people to see colour in a Church context. Everyone was encouraged to wear the appropriate colour for each week – and, by the time they reached Pentecost, the church was a sea of reds.

Over the summer period of seven weeks, the congregation and I explored the colours of the Christian year through themed sermons and activities. In week seven, the theme was centred on 'Colours in our lives as well as our Church!' This was based on Exodus 3:1–15, Matthew 16:13–19 and 'Life in God's Service' in Romans 12, and read from 'The Message' version of the Bible.

Prior to the sermon, 'God believes in YOU!', butterfly pictures were handed out to the congregation.

God believes in YOU!

Over the last few weeks, we have spent time looking at the journey through the Christian year, using colour as our guide. It has been an interesting few weeks, which I hope you have enjoyed.

There is a real richness to our faith that is so often missed in church life. Yet we live in a most beautiful world, full of colour and life. The other day, I was walking my dog, thinking about what we would learn together today, when I saw the most beautiful butterfly. I see lots of Red Admirals and white butterflies on my journeys, but the colours of this butterfly were amazing.

I stopped to admire the wee guy who was sitting on a pile of damp dark mud on the path. I got my phone out of my pocket ready to take a picture, when the movement scared him and he folded up his wings. Now he blended in with the mud. The undersides of his wings were a rich chocolate brown colour, and I could see him only because I knew he was there. He was a Peacock butterfly, found in lowland Scotland – a nettle-lover. And he needs sunshine to be able to fly.

This butterfly brought home to me just how wonderful colour is to our lives. In the midst of the greenery sat this butterfly with bright blue spots, and he stopped me in my tracks. But, since I am the kind of person who is always wondering about things and reflecting on our relationship with God, this butterfly made me think about us as Christians.

> We are all created by God. Amazingly beautiful and
>   intricately made.
> Each of us is like that butterfly.
> Each one of us is loved by God, and we are called to
>   show off our colours.

Two of our readings show God relying on his creation. In the first, Moses, a criminal, a murderer, working with sheep, is called by God to lead the people out of Egypt. Moses says: 'I am a nobody. How can I go to the king and bring the Israelites out of Egypt?'

And then Peter is the rock upon which the Church will be built. Peter is a man of limited education, definitely not diplomatic, and has issues with equality of Jew and Gentile. When you stop and look at just two of the key characters in the Bible whom God has called, then you cannot help but be amazed at whom God can use. I mean, add Paul to the mix, and suddenly you realise that God can use anyone.

And, for the women who might be feeling left out, think of Mary Magdalene, a woman with a dodgy reputation yet the first to meet the risen Christ. Or Mary and Joseph – teenagers blessed with God's child.

Imagine your gifts and personality as colour – just like the colours of the butterfly. Now, if God can work with the likes of Moses, Peter, Paul and Mary and so many others, does it not follow that God can work with us and through us? The great thing is that God does want to work in us and through us. God believes in you. God believes in me – and trust me, I still find that amazing.

The thing is, for many of us, we don't believe that God wants to use us. Or perhaps we are afraid of what might happen if he does. Suddenly, like the butterfly sensing danger, we hide our colours and blend in with our surroundings. We become difficult to spot, and the Church fades from view. Over the generations, the Church has become good at folding her wings and blending in.

But God didn't make us to blend in. He made us full of colour and vibrancy. And he wants us to share that colour and beauty with the world around us.

When Moses said: 'I am a nobody', did God reply: 'Oh yes, bad plan, better find someone else'? NO! God answered: 'I will be with you'.

Or what about Jesus' prophecy about Peter? Jesus said: 'I tell you, Peter: you are a rock, and on this rock foundation I will build my church, and not even death will ever be able to overcome it'.

The peacock butterfly is worthy of one more lesson. The peacock butterfly has striking blue spots that look like eyes – the two top ones being the most vivid. It is another protection element used to scare off predators. It was the blue of these spots that attracted my attention.

Often, answering God's call in our lives is scary. We feel vulnerable, frightened and unsure. When we take a step of faith, we often wonder if it is the right thing to do. Yet, at all times, we are protected by our almighty God. Just as the butterfly is offered protection by his markings, we are marked by God. When Moses faced the king of Egypt, we know that God was with him, in the signs and miraculous events that happened. When Peter failed God by denying Jesus Christ, God was there and brought him back into the fold.

When Paul tried to destroy the Church, God was there, turning the destroyer into the Church's greatest advocate. Remember God loves you, and God believes in you. And there is no higher accolade than knowing that the God who created the universe, right down to the peacock butterfly and beyond, loves you and believes in you.

So today, as we finish our season of colours, think about your colours. Are you willing to show your colours to the world, or do you still want to blend in and hide them?

The peacock butterfly still looked lovely with his wings folded up – but, until he opened them out again, he couldn't fly.

Where might we get to if we all open our colourful wings and trust God to protect us and lead us? Read Romans 12 again for yourself, and pray about showing your colours.   Amen.

Eve

REV. MOYNA McGLYNN

'Eve' was part of a series of six studies, in short-story format, about women in the Bible. It was used for the Church of Scotland Guild Dedication service in 2002. This series was designed to highlight the importance of women in the story of faith. Their mistakes are as real, their devotion as secure, as those of their husbands and sons. The stories were designed to draw upon the experiences of women, their feelings and uncertainties, and to make them alive in the contemporary world by showing that their concerns were the concerns of all women at all times. In worship, the stories affirmed the gifts and insights granted to the women of our congregation, and encouraged everyone in their continuing role in the transmission of faith and in the life of the Church. 'Eve' is the story of an encounter with God who gives significance to all our day-to-day experiences in the world of creation. As such, it is offered as part of this celebratory book.

She straightened her back and scented the air. On the wind, she could smell monkeys, and in the distance she could hear their chattering calls through the trees. She stretched and picked up the grain-filled seed pouch, and headed up the rocks towards the cave-mouth. Usually, monkeys kept away – no more anxious to collide with her than she with them – but sometimes, if there were enough of them, they harried and bullied lone creatures.

She was beginning to notice her weight when she climbed, and she noticed it when she squatted, feet flat on the earth, above the grinding stones. Into the hollowed centre of the lower stone she poured some of the grain, and then she placed the other stone on top and began to turn it slowly, frowning in concentration.

As dusk fell, the Man returned with a small gazelle over his shoulders. He swung it down at her feet while she made crooning noises. Then he went into the cave, rolled himself in skins and slept away his first exhaustion. Meanwhile, she lit a fire, skinned and cooked the meat, and she made flat, hot bread-cakes from the flour she had ground. It was late when she woke the Man to eat. He sat beside her, but took little that night and finally went inside to sleep again. Tomorrow, he would be hungry.

When the moon was at its height, she went to the 'Shining Place', and she waited there for a long time. Through the trees, she could see the fire that burned on the angel's sword. Then the Lord God came from tending his star-beds, and the hem of his robe was living stars, and he wrapped her about like the warmth of the night. And she was afraid of him now, as she had never been, but she was glad that he had come.

She had two small packets with her. One contained the first portion of the meat and the other the first of the bread-cakes. She unwrapped and proffered them.

'Man catch flesh,' she said, 'seed make bread'.

'Excellent', he said. 'Now you must learn to cross the grains and grow them, then you will always have food.' When he spoke, his voice was like the morning song of a thousand wild birds. And he left her then, but the warmth of his presence remained as she crossed the forest floor, barefoot.

Suddenly there was rustling in the bushes, and into the moonlight slipped the green-grey coils of the Snake. Eve and the Snake, perhaps some ten paces apart, looked at each other. Then the Snake began to move away towards the trees, compressing the long line of her scales against the rough ground, the white of her under-belly stained grey-brown by the earth, her eyes coal black with hatred.

It had not always been so. Once she was the most beautiful of all the creatures: her wings were aquamarine, pink and pale yellow, as she hung upon the curtain of the sky. In pride then, and grace, not laboured as now, she had eased her body into the currents, and her back shone like fiery jewels, and perfect was the pale oval of her face, the deep amber glow of her eyes.

But she had lied. She had betrayed the silken words she had learned. And swift and terrible was her fall. Now her wings were shrivelled, and she crawled with effort among the dust. Her tongue was dried, and her melodious voice had become a sharp hiss. Her speech that had charmed, and all her professions of delight, lay broken and maimed and empty between them.

In the morning, Eve woke to the sound of laughter. She hurried out to see. The Man was awake and naked in the river. With his cupped hands he had caught a fish, and it flapped this way and that. Close to the bank, he threw the fish and it landed on the stones, still flapping. In the water, he seemed taller and his skin glowed as though it were oiled. Drops of water had run through his curling hair, and they hung like small jewels on his face. His eyes were still alive with laughter. It was a long time, a very long time, since she had heard him laugh. To cover the tears that suddenly blinded her, she scooped up the fish, making clicking, disapproving noises with her tongue.

For what seemed like weeks, they made tools. They cut tall, straight branches, and stripped them of bark and rubbed them smooth with rough stones and handfuls of sand. Then they collected flint boulders and dropped them from a high ledge until they split open, revealing their smooth, metallic, ink-black flesh. With broken chips, the Man cut wedge-shaped blades and bound them to the branches with plaited fibres.

For what seemed like weeks, they cleared the ground, cutting down the wild foliage and setting fire to the stubble. Sometimes the Man would disappear for a few days and return with a fresh kill. Sometimes Eve would smell the ripeness of wild fruit, and she would go and gather soft berries to crush and bruise into a pulpy drink, or she would come upon a cluster of stone-like nut shells, hiding the creamy sweetness inside. Sometimes they ate fish from the river. From the nuts they made oil.

Then one day, they were ready to sow. The Man stood with his long-handled blade at the edge of the cleared ground, and Eve was behind with mixed wild seeds in a pouch. He smiled at her, and drove the blade deep into the earth, and wherever it bit, it drove spumes of loamy, black soil into banks at the sides of the runnel. Eve walked along the runnel, letting the seeds slip through her fingers. Every few paces, they stopped and covered the seed with the banked earth, while the following birds called in thwarted fury.

After that, things were easier for a while. Apart from the days of the hunting trips, there was little to do but wait and eat. Eve took the bloodied pelts of their prey down to the river to wash them clean. Then she staked them out to dry in the sun. They would make clothes for the winter. But winter seemed a long way off in those mellow days as summer ended. They gathered fruit, wild onions and marrow, and stored them in the cool of the cave. Eve dragged out the skins on which they slept, and spread them out on the rock ledge. Then she beat them with a bundle of sticks to get rid of the dust. She knew she was getting ready. Her movements were slowing now.

Then one morning they awoke, and the cleared field was a carpet of tiny shoots. So beautiful did it seem, that Eve went in and out of the cave, each time to be surprised by the wave of soft green above the dark patches of earth. The Man was pleased too, and he walked carefully between the runnels, occasionally stooping to unfurl the miniature leaves of each perfect plant.

But then the woes came. First it remained too hot, and some of the plants baked and turned brown in the sun. Then, when the rain came, it beat and battered against the upright stalks, and they bent with the weight of it. Eve and the Man watched anxiously.

Some sprang back as soon as the heavy rain ceased; some had been uprooted and lay withered on the dark ground. Each torn plant gave a kind of pain.

Then, when the remaining stalks measured the span of two hands, they awoke one morning to see a strange dust-cloud far off. By midday it had blotted out the sun, and the sky was dark and angry. The Man was clearly uneasy, and he made sharp noises if she moved from the cave mouth, even when she went to the riverbank to fill a gourd shell with water.

A few hours after midday, the first outriders of the cloud fell to the ground outside the cave. They were three times the size of a grasshopper, with powerful jaws. At first, Eve stared at them blindly; then it began to rain large grasshoppers, and from the left and the right they fell from the sky. The Man pulled Eve inside the cave; and outside, where the light came, they watched the storm as it passed: the churning of the fetid, brown air; the strange buzz of a million beating wings. When the sound finally died away, they went outside and surveyed the ruin of their valley.

The evening was mild, the sun rosy and still quite high on the horizon, although in the far valleys the shadows were beginning to lengthen. Everywhere, the ground was polluted with the carcases of insects, and some stragglers still living, trying to fly away to die elsewhere. Not a leaf remained on a tree or bush: every branch was stripped, and, where the young grain field had stood with its neat rows of waving plants, there was nothing, only the dun-grey of the bitten earth. The Man stood clenching and unclenching his hands, and then he gave a howl of despair and turned and walked away through the scoured clearing. Eve tried to run after him, and she called: 'Adam, Adam', and he returned, shocked at the use of a name long unused, and Eve cradled him in the white rage of his disappointment while the Snake, bloated from feeding, uncoiled herself from among the rocks and watched them.

Eventually he slept, and, as he did, the lines of taut strain fell from his face. His skin was smooth, his curling beard glossy, the arc of his dark eyelashes creating purple shadows along the line of his cheek.

And Eve got up and went to the 'Shining Place', taking a little oil and a fresh bread-cake. Through the trees, she could see the fire that burned on the angel's sword. She waited for a long time. Then the Lord God came from the sources of the rivers, and the hem of his robe was the tumbling waters, and he wrapped her about with cool, soothing streams. And she was afraid of him now, as she had never been, but she was glad that he had come.

'Grasshoppers came', she said, opening and shutting her mouth in imitation of their jaws, 'Field gone. Adam –' she tried to remember words, 'heart break'.

'No, no', he said. 'It will not break. It will mend. When Spring comes, you must begin again. Did you collect and store food as I told you?'

'Yes,' she said, 'wild fruit stored, vegetables stored, grain stored.'

'Good,' he said, 'and you may plant the vegetable seeds also. And, if you need anything, you can come here to this place. There is fruit and grain here. Be comforted.' And his voice was like the lulling of the waves of the sea, and all the strength of gathered waters, and he was gone from her, but the cool balm of his presence stayed with her as she made her way over the forest floor.

In the morning, the valley had been washed clean with rain, and the river tumbled with brown water rushing down from the hills. The very air seemed alive with water. Adam went hunting. He was away for longer than usual, and Eve fretted and went continually to the cave-mouth, hoping to see him return. After four days he came, white with tiredness and bearing a young stag. He was bowed under its weight, and the muscles of his neck and arms stood out with the intense effort of carrying it up to the cave from the tracks below.

Eve cut the meat into pieces. Some she cooked and some she hung. The skin was scraped clean. It was as she was finishing, perhaps it had begun sooner, that she was aware of a turning in her belly, and the muscles seemed to lock. Birth she had seen: she-monkeys running through the clearing, wild goats upon the hills; of this rising and falling pain she knew nothing. In the event, it did not take long. The child arrived, red and angry and bawling, and it was Adam who cut him free and then sat watching her, a strange look in his eyes. And Eve, drifting between exhaustion and euphoria, looked at her son. He had long-arched lashes and silky patches of damp hair. His eyes, when he scrutinised her face, were pools of black. Several times she woke in the night and remembered with sudden shock that he was there.

All the next day, she lay in a warm cocoon only shattered, periodically, by the child's cries. Adam fetched her water and food. There was a slightly bewildered look about him now, as though he was puzzled that the child was still there.

'Cain,' he said at last, 'Cain'. So the child had a name. He was Cain. And both she and Adam turned away from each other, so that they would not remind each other by the merest sign of that other naming day.

It had been in the full flood of summer, the evening stirred by a soft breeze. They sat beside the river as the animals came to drink. They came in a hundred colours. They came with stripes and printed markings, hide plates, coats coarse, coats soft; or shell-like armour. They had white or cream underbellies, tails held high, or no tails, eyes green or orange. They loped, or ran, or crawled, or flew in bright flashes. They had trunks, or tusks, or claws, or speed, or bounding leaps. They came disguised, in camouflage, like the stippled patches of sunlight, like the tall waving grasses, like the leaves of a tree, like bark sticks, like budding flowers. They were bustling and busy, lazy and leisurely. They came one by one – and he named them all, as the evening turned to dusk.

And they drank wine made from berries fermented with honey, and they poured it into goblets of baked, glazed clay, painted bright greens and yellows like the wings of the parakeets. Over some names they had argued, and over others they had laughed. The Snake was the best at thinking them up. She could make up words in an instant, words that evoked a lumbering gait, an effortless stroll, words which took account of their chatter, words which drew out their most unusual feature. She was gifted with words, and her voice had been full of lilting and laughter.

When they were all named, the Snake made up a song and sang it in the last shadows when the stars were appearing. It was heart-breakingly beautiful. Adam sang the counter-point, and just when the Snake had lifted herself into the wind, the Lord God came from the song of the planets, and the music he brought was the symphony of creation, and the hem of his robe was the soft echoes of all the scales of the universe. It had been a good day – one of the best. But the memory now brought only sorrow, and the vivid picture of the Snake pulling her coils over the bracken, silently.

The world has wounds, Eve thought, from betrayal. And she glanced down at her sleeping child, suddenly afraid for him. Yet, because she loved him, she knew that love was still there.

That winter was hard, with little enough to eat. Wild goats came down from the hills, followed swiftly by the wolves. Adam had found a she-goat that had gone lame and had brought it home, thinking to tether it and have the milk. But the wolves killed it in the night and left its carcase livid against the snow. The wolves became so hungry that they began to hang around the cave-mouth at night, and Eve was terrified for the baby and scared to let Adam go to hunt. They kept the fire alight at night, and they ate the grain seeds they had hoped to plant in the spring.

Adam seemed curiously content, not restless, as Eve had feared. He had begun to make tools again, mending and sharpening those that were worn, modifying those that had worked less well than he had hoped, experimenting with new designs. He made an implement, with a long, light shaft and a narrow blade. Eve saw him balancing its weight in his hand. Then he stood at the cave-mouth and hurled it towards a tree some sixty paces away.

For one second he stood, his body taut with concentration, feet firmly apart, one just a little in front of the other taking the weight. And, as all the gathered momentum threw him forward, he released the shaft, and the blade whistled and thudded into the tree. Then he was full of excitement. Nothing would do but to do it over and over again. But Eve understood it all. No longer would he have to run down his prey when hunting. Now, provided his aim was accurate, he could stand at a distance and bring down the animal he had selected. And his aim would be accurate. She could tell by the assurance of his movements, by the confidence in his eyes.

Soon after, the thaw came with the same intensity of brightness that had brought the iron winter. The river outside the cave was in spate, tossing its brackish water against the rocks. The wolves retreated. Adam went hunting with his new tool and returned the same day with a goat. When Eve began to skin it, she saw it had a long gash in its breast, cut clean through to the bone. Her child was becoming more mobile, not walking, but he could sit and stretch, and Eve kept him strapped to her with a long pelt, for fear of the fire, and the river, and a thousand nameless things.

They went looking for new grain in the finger of a valley between the hills. They were lucky. There were stalks of wheat and heavier barley growing at random among the weeds and the ferns. They pulled the heads from each stalk, then rolled the heads between their hands until the seeds came away. Slowly, as they worked, the seed pouches grew heavier.

It was a cloudy afternoon with a slight chill in the air, the kind of day that looks mild but has a hidden rawness. Away in the distance, they could see bands of rain striking another hillside, but where they were was sheltered and it remained dry. They were undisturbed and the baby slept, warm against his mother's back.

Eve pulled away a curtain of grass, and nestling behind it was a small vine with a cluster of stunted grapes. How the vine had survived such a bitter winter, she could not know. She was about to call Adam, when she realised with a shock that the grapes were not wild but cultivated. For a second she stared about her wildly, trying to find something familiar in the landscape but failing to recognise any of it. The hillsides sloped in descending steps – the terraces? This wild, overgrown mayhem!

And then, as she rounded a small spur, she saw the gorge and the cluster of five trees. They were bare now, only the merest swelling of the buds on the overgrown stems showing a hint of the life that had blossomed while they sat, eating roasted guinea fowl, and sherbet and almonds, and the trees, drowsy with their weighted beauty, rained petals on their hair and shoulders.

She looked across at Adam. He was perhaps thirty, forty paces away, moving along the valley where the trees would be hidden from his view. There was a rhythm in the way he stooped, straightened, rolled the grain, dropped the seeds into his pouch and let the air take the dry chaff. There was an economy of movement, a suppressed and athletic energy. As if sensing her gaze, he looked up, vaguely smiling. And she realised that he was not made for leisure, but for struggle and triumphs by his own wiry frame – by the sweat of his brow. She began to pull the grain, moving in a line towards him, and they walked home, carrying the straining pouches.

They marked out the corners of the field and set fire to the weeds. A few days later, they began to plough again, once more seeing the spumes of black earth rise from the blade like small jets of water, once more placing the smooth brown kernels into the run and covering them protectively. Adam sang a song as he worked, in a rich, deep voice. It was a song of paradise. It was the first time that he had sung since they came to the cave.

Imperceptibly, it was spring. Buds thick with sticky sap appeared on the branches. The first flowers appeared in clumps of blues and yellows. The river was full of leaping, darting fish, which Adam sometimes speared. Cain's limbs were rounded and fat, and in the field, the ranks of grain shoots were daily taller.

Eve baked bread. Then she took a small, freshly caught fish, cooked it and wrapped it. She took also a piece of sweet honeycomb. When she had prepared these things, she strapped the baby to her back, and went to the 'Shining Place'. In the distance, she could see the dull glow of the angel's sword. She waited for a long time. Then the Lord God came from the molten fires of the earth's core, and the hem of his robe was a seam of topaz and a seam of gold, and he wrapped her about with a white sheen of silver. She was in awe of him now, but she was glad that he had come.

She offered him the food – and she sat, letting the waves of well-being fill her senses.

Eventually, she said: 'Garden still here – weeds – broken'.

'Yes,' he said.

And she looked down at her son, wrapped in his warm pelt in the long grass at her feet. He was drowsy with milk, not quite sleeping and not quite awake.

'And love still here,' she said, 'love makes pain now.'

'Yes,' he said.

And she thought of Adam, driving the flint blade into the earth and singing his song of paradise. 'Glory still here', she said. 'Garden, love, glory, all still here. Sometimes see, sometimes not see.'

'Yes,' he replied. 'You must look for them all the time – this is life.'

And his voice was like the shimmer of hazy sunshine, reaching down, healing, and like the crackle of new fire moving brightly from twig to twig. And he was gone from her, but the warmth of his presence remained with her as she walked, sure-footed, over the shifting plates of the earth.

The Parable of the Prodigal Daughter

REV. ANNE LOGAN

This sermon is a contemporary take on a familiar parable and was preached on Mother's Day at which the Girls' Brigade was present.

Last year, we went to visit one of my cousins. He lives in a pretty little tourist village in the north of England. There's now a bypass round it, so it's quiet again. You know the kind of place, little yellow brick houses hanging on to the hillside, stepping up the street. The doors open onto the street, and the gardens are all to the back. There's a post office that sells sweets and cards, tea, sugar and toilet rolls. 'The Black Swan' specialises in real ale and home-cooked food.

Cousin and I went for a stroll before dinner. We walked to the top of the village, and there on the outskirts was a big house set back from the road, with what had been fine lawns stretched out in front of it. The outbuildings at the back had scaffolding. Some kind of renovation project had started – but the whole thing was boarded up, deserted. 'What happened,' I asked, 'did they run out of money?' 'Not exactly', came the reply; and he told me the story.

'I don't know when the family came to the village, but when we moved here, Joy ran the house as a hotel-cum-guesthouse. She lived there with her two girls, Jane and Juliet. Juliet was a pretty wee girl: all long blonde hair and big eyes, she knew how to get round people. As a wee girl, she would just run up to someone and give them a hug – and everybody loved her, petted her and gave her sweeties. By the time she was ten, she was spoiled rotten and a real little madam, but she had a pretty smile, and people just laughed and said: "that's just Juliet". The sister was older, not ugly or anything, just an ordinary kid. Very serious, though, and forever running after her sister, telling her not to eat so many sweeties, or that it was time to go home, or that she shouldn't hug strangers. But Jane had very little success, and Juliet just did her own thing.

'As Juliet grew up, she was stunning and she knew it. Every time she strutted down the village, she had a male audience, and she loved it. She always had the latest clothes and shoes – you've never seen such a collection of shoes. The tale in the village was that she had over 200 pairs of shoes.'

We walked on for a bit, while I tried to figure out how to store 200 pairs of shoes. But then, Cousin began the story again.

'Juliet was still at school at the time, and we used to wonder how she could afford the shoes, not to mention the clothes and the make-up. Every time she got off the bus on a Saturday, she was festooned with shopping. But one time, I was behind her mum, Joy, in the post office when she took out her purse to pay for the groceries and burst into tears because there was no money in her purse. Of course she covered up, but it was obvious that Juliet had emptied her purse before going off to town that morning. Then it got worse: she stole her mother's bank card and emptied the account, she "borrowed" the credit card and ran up huge bills, but by now it wasn't shoes and make-up she was after. Every time you saw her, she was so spaced out she couldn't hold a conversation. Then one day, she just disappeared. Told her mother and her sister that she wasn't staying in this dead-end place any longer, and just went. She went off to Manchester to see some 'action', she said. Joy phoned her, texted her, but eventually the phone was cut off. Juliet was away to the streets in Manchester; there was nothing she wouldn't do for money, nothing she wouldn't do for her next fix. Every Sunday, her mother went off to Manchester to look for her. Every time, she came back defeated.

'Meantime, the elder daughter, Jane, proved to be a real trouper. She'd worked hard at school and had gone on to do hotel management at the local college. She got up the ladders and redecorated the hotel, she improved the marketing and put them on the Internet. She went away for a few weeks on a specialist cookery course and came back and revamped the menu. The hotel was great, we'd all go there for nights out, and people came to it from all over. Joy was the life and soul of the place – a really warm, friendly woman. Jane was always the same, deadly serious. A bit bitter and sour, really. Joy did the up-front stuff and Jane slaved away behind the scenes, but it was a great success.'

'So, what happened after that?' I asked.

'Juliet came back after a phone call from the police one night. She was in intensive care in Manchester. One of her clients had beaten her up, and she was in a bad way. Joy brought her home, looked after her and paid for her to attend a residential clinic to get rid of the drugs.

'When she finally came back, she was the old Juliet, happy, pretty, charming. Joy was absolutely thrilled. "It's a miracle!" she kept telling us. "It's as though she's come back from the dead!" '

Cousin went on: 'Joy decided to convert the outhouses at the back into self-catering units. Bob, the local joiner, started work on them. But Joy said to Jane that she was going to give the self-catering units to Juliet so that she could run them and earn her keep. It would give her something to do and bring her a bit of money. Jane lost it totally. She ranted and raved. "I've been here all this time! I've turned this hotel around! I've worked! I've slaved! I've scrimped and saved! I've done everything for you – but are you giving *me* the cottages? Oh no! You aren't giving me anything! Why is it all going to lady Juliet, the one who wasted everything she ever had?"

'Jane rampaged through the dining room, throwing the crockery on the floor. Her mother ran after her, saying: "The hotel is yours, Jane, you know that it's left to you in my will". But Jane stormed upstairs, packed her bags and sent for a taxi. She went off to London and got a fantastic job in one of the big hotels. A few weeks later, Joy closed the hotel and had it boarded up, and she and Juliet went off to London after Jane.'

'So how did it all end?' I asked. 'Are they all together now?' Cousin Peter reached out to open the front gates of his house and said: 'I've absolutely no idea'.

Section 6
All-Age Worship

The Big Red Bike

REV. JILL CLANCY

Although I have no children, I am a step-mum, a step-gran and an aunt and still have a gran who is now 95 years of age. My story about Elliot has been used in church, primary schools and residential homes.

The big story: Luke 11:10–13

The little story:

Let me tell you about a wee boy called Elliot – not an Elliot you know, but an Elliot I know. Elliot was about six years of age, and he had a neighbour called Jack who was five years of age and a class below Elliot at school. The boys were good friends but only ever got to play together in the evenings or at weekends because, even though they went to the same school together, they played in different playgrounds because Jack was only in Primary 1 and Elliot was going into Primary 3.

So, when Elliot got home from school, he would come in, see his mum, drink the milk and eat the sandwich his mum had made for him, get his homework done and hopefully within half an hour he would be out in the cul-de-sac at his house playing with Jack.

The boys played well together, but Elliot really, really loved playing with Jack's wee red car. Elliot always asked Jack for a go, and he would drive around the cul-de-sac loving every minute of his go on Jack's wee red car.

Now, Elliot's birthday was coming up – he was going to be seven, although he never looked his age because he was small in stature, but nonetheless seven he would be. And so, one night while mum was getting him ready for bed, she asked him: 'Elliot, what would you like for your seventh birthday?' 'Well,' Elliot said, 'I don't even need to think about it, because I know what I want, what I really, really want for my birthday, and that is a wee red car like Jack's. Please, mum, can I have a wee red car like Jack's? 'Well,' said mum, 'we'll see.'

That night, when Elliot went to bed, he started to say his prayers, as he always did, but that night he asked God if he could make sure that he got a wee red car like Jack's for his birthday.

Now, Elliot's birthday was a whole month away at that time, but every night while mum was getting him ready for bed, he would tell her over and over again what he wanted for his birthday, 'Please, mum, I really want a wee red car like Jack's. Please, mum, can I get it for my birthday?' And every night during his prayers, he prayed hard to God that he would make sure that his mum and dad bought him a wee red car like Jack's for his birthday. And so this went on every night for a whole month UNTIL the morning of his birthday came along.

Elliot was so excited he could hardly sleep, and instead of mum dragging him out of bed at eight o'clock Elliot was up, face washed, teeth cleaned and clothes on by 7:30am, and he was running downstairs to see if his birthday present was there, his wee red car like Jack's.

Well, when he got downstairs his mum hugged him and wished him a very happy birthday, but then as Elliot stood waiting to be shown where his present was, his mum said that she had lots of presents for him, from his gran, his aunts, his cousins, even his friends, which he could open up there and then, but that Elliot would have to wait until daddy came home from work that night before he would get his main present from them.

Well, Elliot turned around a little deflated and started opening up his presents. He got some money in cards, he got some new pyjamas from Gran, some T-shirts from his cousins, an Action Man from his aunt, but his heart just wasn't in those presents; he just wanted to see his wee red car like Jack's.

It came to 8:50am, and it was time to go to school. His mum waved him goodbye at the playground gates, and off Elliot went to class. But what a day he had – he just couldn't concentrate at all, he talked too much, he day-dreamed constantly; and his teacher, even though it was his birthday, felt as if she was always giving him trouble. 'Elliot, stop looking out of the window. Elliot, would you please do as you are told? Elliot, can you at least listen to what I am saying?' So, as you can imagine, when the bell went at three o'clock, Elliot was thrilled, and he was the first out of the class – backpack on, coat on, inside out, shoes on, but on the wrong feet – and off he ran to jump in mum's car, hoping that daddy would be home early because Elliot wanted to get out to play on his new wee red car just like Jack's.

'Is dad home yet?', Elliot asked his mum. 'No, Elliot, he won't be home until 6pm tonight, but don't worry, you'll have a birthday tea then, because gran and grandad, your aunt Agnes and Uncle Norrie will all be there waiting for you, and you will be able to blow your candles out on your favourite of all cakes, your chocolate birthday cake.'

But even all this news of his birthday tea just meant nothing to Elliot, because he wanted to see his new wee red car. Tea came and went, and Elliot watched the clock tick round every second until it came to 6pm – and so, as he stood at the front window looking out, he thought if dad didn't drive round that corner within the next few minutes he would just burst, and just at that he saw dad's car.

Elliot was at the front door waiting for dad to walk up the path. He got a huge hug from dad and was delighted to see his dad then leave Elliot in the living room and go to the garage to get his present.

It was a big box, bigger than Elliot had imagined the car would come in. He ripped the paper off the box in such a fashion that his mum was looking a little annoyed at all the mess on the carpet, and under the paper was a brown box, oh how excited Elliot was, his own wee red car just like Jack's – he couldn't wait, and so he opened up the box and took out …

A BIG RED BIKE, with stabilisers!!!!

This was not what Elliot had asked for every night before his birthday; this was not what he had prayed for every night before his birthday. This was not a wee red car like Jack's; it was a BIG RED BIKE.

'Well,' his dad said, 'do you like it?' 'Yes', said Elliot not very enthusiastically. His dad saw that Jack was outside, and said to Elliot: 'Well, son, on you go and see Jack there, he'll be thrilled to see your new bike'. Elliot didn't think so, but went out anyway.

'Hi Jack', said Elliot. 'Hi Elliot, happy birthday', said Jack. 'Hey, is that bike your birthday present?' 'Yes', said Elliot, even less enthusiastically than before. 'Oh, it's fantastic, can I have a go?' asked Jack. 'Yeah, sure.' And so off Jack went round the cul-de-sac on Elliot's new big red bike. He loved it, it made him feel like a big boy, and he was so happy for Elliot.

Elliot and Jack continued to play until the sun started going down that night and mum called Elliot in for his bath. They had a great time, and most afternoons after school the two of them would be found out playing in the cul-de-sac with Jack's wee red car and Elliot's big red bike. And a few months later, the only thing the boys played with was Elliot's big red bike because neither Jack nor Elliot could fit into Jack's wee red car any more.

Then, a few months after that, the stabilisers were taken off Elliot's bike – and do you know what Jack got for his birthday? A brand new Big Blue Bike!!

(After you tell the story your way, you then expand on the big story on how God knows what's best for us, and so if we pray for something and we think that it hasn't been answered the way we have wanted it to be answered, we may just find that it has been answered perfectly because God knows what we need, just as Elliot's mum and dad knew what he

needed and knew that buying Elliot a wee red car would have been no use, and a big red bike would last him a lot longer and was the best present in the long run …)

If the Hat Fits!

REV. CHRISTINE CREEGAN

This Mothers' Day address was used in church and Grandtully School, where it worked well. The surprise element and the participation of the children were good, and it could be adapted and used for Fathers' Day. It could also be used as a celebration of women.

Today is a very special day. It is the day set aside for saying 'thank you' to mothers.

This day was called Refreshment Sunday, because it came halfway through Lent. The Church decided people needed a break from the fasting of Lent. It was a day that people were given as a holiday to enable them to travel home to their 'mother' church. For some, it was the only day they would see their families.

The way we celebrate Mother's Day now is influenced by America. On 9 May 1906, a lady called Anna Jarvis lost her mother. On the first anniversary of her mother's death, she decided that a day should be set aside to honour all mothers. So, in America, this day is celebrated on the second Sunday in May.

Why should we say 'thank you' to mothers?

Because they do so much for us – they wear many different hats. For example (*at this point, produce bag filled with the following, and pull out one at a time*):

> **Chef's hat** – cooking meals
> **Bowler hat** – looking after the finances like a bank manager
> **Nurse's hat** – healing cuts with a plaster

Policeman's hat – keeping law and order in the home
   between brothers and sisters
Clown's hat – keeping children amused
Fancy wedding hat – when mother has to be glamorous
(*Other hats may be added*)

We need to say thank you to mothers for wearing all these hats at different times. We also have to remember to say thank you to God for all his goodness to us.

The children really enjoy waiting to see the next hat that comes out of the bag. And they might just enjoy 'modelling' them as each one appears!

Kids in Kirk

REV. CHRISTINE SIME

KIK worked very well because of its ongoing commitment to children and supporting their parents in the baptismal vows they had made. This ministry from birth until Sunday School age addresses a gap and a need in many churches.

Over the years of the Church of Scotland's 'Church Without Walls' project, Dunscore congregation had been watching for opportunities in church and community – watching not only for gaps, but also for ideas to help fill voids, not least in our own church worship.

Ask (almost) any church what they would really like, and the chances are that somewhere would be a prayer for young families, young children, to be part of the life of the church. We have not cracked this by any stretch of anyone's imagination, but here is one idea we have tried. The idea is not mind-blowing, rather mind-blowingly simple.

I would not describe Dunscore church as active – that term depicts an all too sedentary pace. We have amazing people – elders, board members and so-called lay members who are eager, and willing, to give of their time. And it was from such a group that this idea grew. They brainstormed around our children's needs. They wanted to find a way to help us all to maintain the congregation's baptismal vow to look after the children in our midst.

We have a small Sunday School – but Sunday mornings are not always the best times. We have a very small crèche facility, but still under-threes are sparse. What do children love? What would bring them out?

A party! And so, a Party in the Park was organised. All the under-eight-year-olds in the church, and in the parish, were invited personally.

In a small village, we have the benefit of good relations with other groups. The pre-school building, beside the park, agreed to open its doors for toilets! So that was the main concern catered for.

A clown was booked (and that cost was paid willingly). On the morning of our party, it rained; but by lunchtime the sun had come through, and with over fifty youngsters and their families we were entertained, we ran around the park and had fun. Two local pipers arrived to pipe us all the few hundred yards, watched by villagers cheering and waving, through the middle of the village to the church, where a transformation had taken place. Helium balloons split the space between the floor and the very high ceiling. There were picnic rugs where chairs had been, and tables laden with party food lined the back wall.

Many parents had never been 'in church' before – and they were amazed.

Some of our own regular members were just as amazed!

At the end of the day, we, the church, had put on a day to remember (for free), and we ourselves had also been able to see not only that the families and children were around, but also that they were willing to come – somewhere, sometime.

The follow-up has been services held every six to eight weeks designed for the under-eights.

Invitations are sent out, and a planning meeting convened. The 'organisers' change as people can or cannot manage. We pick a theme and build a short service held on a Sunday at 3pm and lasting around twenty-five minutes – long enough for that age group.

We learned (or *I* did) the following from the first attempt:

- At 4pm, it was too late for many – tea and bath times approached too fast.

- It was too long and too complicated, and the leaders (myself especially) were too nervous, in fact terrified. But we have discovered a format that, for the moment, works, with around twelve to fifteen under-eights coming each time.

Themes and activities have been:

- Feeding of the 5,000 – songs, story and with each picnic rug having a picnic basket filled with dolls' picnic gear plus the odd car etc. added to keep the boys amused. I did wonder if they had heard any of the story as they played, but I was surprised by their ability to multi-task – one wee three-year-old had apparently told a neighbour ALL about it.

- Near Harvest, we persuaded a few of our gentlemen to build us a tent in one corner of the church. They loved doing it, and the kids were enthralled. We marched round the church, as the people of Israel going to the Promised Land; we disappeared into the tent from where, a few at a time, messengers were sent out to find food. Back they came with their wee baskets full of manna (popcorn).

- The Christmas-time service avoided the word, but talked about the arrival of a baby. They found clothes and toys, and we discovered a crib just behind the Communion table, where a few of the girls immediately began to redress the baby doll. Story cubes were used to tell the story.

- Jesus 'lost' at the Temple involved one elder telling with great actions the story of the time her daughter had been 'lost' (left behind) at a bookshop. We had a treasure hunt for soft toys, hearts and wee books.

- Palm Sunday looms – all we know is that we have a wonderful model donkey, that there will be the usual helium balloon, and juice with raisins after the service. (One point we had to be careful with was not giving sweets, biscuits and the like. Raisins keep the parents on side!)

Actual practicalities – it does need to be planned, but the content does not have to be very much, nor very complex. The planning meetings are in fact wonderful fun, when we all get to think small and silly – and considering worship for the under-eights helps us get to grips with the real point of the passage. When folk are arriving, there needs to be some activity or singing to join in with, and we have discovered that a brief résumé of what will happen not only helps the parents know what it is all about, but also alerts them to the times when help may be required to march youngsters round the church, to gather them in to open their baskets or boxes, or to help them find treasures.

A story, something to 'discover' from a box or basket, an activity, songs, and a final prayer to round it all off. And then they explore the church, they get to know the building and the people. Another wall broken down for children and their families.

Planning for the first service was already complete when we realised we did not have a name, a heading for posters and invitations. We decided on the name on the Church of Scotland material *Kids in Kirk* – KIK.

These services give us a great reason to keep in touch with baptismal families – no matter where they are. Invitations go around the country, contact is maintained, and you never know when they might be visiting the area again.

And it helps the congregation to feel that they are at least doing something to keep the vow they make at baptisms – looking after the children in their midst.

Another party is planned – a chance to reconvene, gather in others and, of course, have fun.

The Other Duckling

REV. MARY HENDERSON

'The Other Duckling' was first used at Bridge Foundation Conference in 1999 on the theme of 'The Ugly Duckling', which was about personal growth and self-realisation. It has 'good entertainment value' but also encourages people to think about the fairy story in the context of faith. Are we only acceptable to God if there is a spectacular transformation, or are we loved as we are? It is particularly relevant to women, whose self-image is often poor.

You all know the story of the Ugly Duckling. But I'm almost sure you won't know about the Other Duckling, because I made him up – and here he is!

A long, long time had passed since Hans Christian Andersen had told the world about the Ugly Duckling who was really a royal swan. Not only human children but also baby ducklings were told the story while they were still in the nest, and it was one of their favourites because it made them feel so important. Maybe one day they too would turn into a beautiful swan.

And the mummy ducks who were telling the story, and knew it was just a story really, would still look very carefully at their eggs to see if there was one that was bigger and darker than the rest. Most of them were very careful not to call any of their ducklings UGLY just in case there was another swan that had got into the nest by mistake.

And so it happened, in a pond just outside [*home town*], that the Other Duckling was born.

The egg hatched out at just the right time; and the chick looked just the same as all his brothers and sisters. No-one laughed at him or chased him away. Everything was going just fine, in fact, until it came to STORY TIME one day, and his mummy duck told the story of the Ugly Duckling. 'Once upon a time, there was a family of ducks ...'

The Other Duckling listened, entranced, and when it came to the end he thought: 'Wow! That's me! I knew it! That explains everything! Why, I'm so much more beautiful ... so much cleverer than all these other ducklings. I'm not a duck at all. I'm far more special. I'm a Royal Swan.'

From that moment onwards, he never went paddling with the other ducks. He practised GLIDING smoothly over the water. He never dived for worms; he never uttered another QUACK – because he knew that swans were strong and silent.

He was a bit LONELY, especially when the other ducks started laughing and making fun of him, but after all, wasn't that what was supposed to happen? It really just confirmed that he was right: he was different ... he was special ... he was a ROYAL SWAN.

Then, one day, he went swimming to the other side of the duckpond and saw what he had been waiting for: two pure white adult swans with their little brown cygnets following on behind.

His little heart gave a leap – he almost QUACKED out loud for joy, but he remembered just in time that he was a swan, and he glided as smoothly as he knew how up to the swans, waiting for them to turn round and welcome him home.

But when the Daddy Swan turned round and saw the Other Duckling, he hissed angrily and told him to go away. The Mummy Swan didn't open her soft white wings to give him a cuddle. The Baby Swans didn't want to play with him, but still he glided along behind them at a safe distance (as smoothly as a duckling can) because he was so sure that he was really a Royal Swan.

As the days went by, he got sadder and lonelier (secretly he wished he was back with the other ducklings), but he kept gliding along on his own. He had got used to the other ducklings laughing whenever they met, so he paid no attention to them, and almost didn't notice when a new little duck came by.

She was a very pretty girl duck (with a pink bow); what was strange was that she wasn't laughing or pointing her beak at him. She was quacking 'HELLO' – and when he turned away, looking regal, a little salty tear plopped out of her eye into the water – because she thought he was the handsomest, coolest, fittest boy duck she had ever seen.

She swam up closer and said: 'Hello, little duck. Why are you swimming with the swans; why don't you come with me to dunk for worms?'

And the Other Duckling said, a little more hesitantly: 'Can't you see? I'm a SWAN.'

And, at that, DAISY (that was the girl duck's name) started quacking with laughter. But it wasn't the cruel laughter of the other ducklings – it was kind. 'Don't be daft', she said. 'You're the cutest, coolest, fittest duck I've ever seen – and I fancy you something rotten!'

And, at that moment, the Other Duckling forgot all about the Swans, and about being Royal and different: he did a triple somersault back-flip duck roll and quacked for all he was worth for the whole pond to hear; and he swam over to Daisy, and they got married, and the next spring they had little ducklings of their own, and told them lots of stories, but never ever the story of the ugly duckling.

Who Loves Ya, Baby?

REV. ELSIE FORTUNE

I enjoy the challenge of creating children's addresses. 'Who Loves Ya, Baby?' is a different 'take' on the Good Samaritan, and its contemporary has worked well.

The props for this address can be found throughout the script. Interaction with the children comes from them identifying the characters and saying WHO they are.

I have a packet of Jelly Babies here – let me tell a story of what happened to one of them.

The Jelly Baby (JB) goes for a stroll in the countryside, and sits down to have a picnic, when who comes along? – **a Drifter** (WHO? – describe for me) – someone who wanders from place to place, up to no good. He upsets the picnic, steals JB's money, beats him up and leaves him for dead.

Some time later, along comes **a Bounty (Hunter)** (WHO? – describe for me) – someone who tracks down people who have done something wrong and receives money for taking them to the authorities. He asks if JB has seen anyone suspicious going about. Weakly, JB raises an arm and points in the direction the **Drifter** went. The **Bounty Hunter** thanks him as he races off.

Some time later, along comes **Mr Polo Mint** (WHO? – describe for me) – so pure and white. Will he help Jelly Baby? NO! He's so saintly but so empty inside, caring only for himself. And he passes by.

Some time later, along comes **Miss Sour Lemon** (WHO? – describe for me) – she's got out of the bed on the wrong side, and is so grumpy and sour that she does not have time to stop and help.

Some time later, along comes **the Marsh Mallow** – soft-hearted, weak, who can't even bear to look at JB's injuries (WHO? – describe for me) – and passes on. He's just so soft.

Some time later, along comes **Mr Toffo** (WHO? – describe for me) – so full of self-importance, head and nose in the air (toffee-nosed), that he does not even see JB.

Some time later, along come **the Milky Bar Kid**, **Mr Crunchie** and **Mrs Mars** (WHO? – describe for me) – **Milky Bar Kid** – strong and tough, **Crunchie** – heart of gold, and **Mrs Mars** – works, rests and plays.

They stop and help JB. They telephone for a **Taxi** – escort him to Accident and Emergency, make sure he is taken care of – and leave their e-mail address, telephone number and cheque card to help out.

Who Loves Ya, Baby? Who is your neighbour?

The story used JB as a universal figure of many colours. Alternatively, for older groups, other main characters can be used: for example, a Big Issue *vendor on his early-morning corner spot.*

29,000 Plastic Ducks

REV. ALISON JACK

This worship material was used in July 2005 at the end-of-term service at Simon Langton School for Girls, Canterbury. Preaching in Canterbury Cathedral was an awe-inspiring occasion, but the best bit was looking out at a sea of girls' faces, all (or mostly all!) listening intently to hear the story of the globe-trotting ducks. It's an exciting adventure story just right for an end-of-term service, when everyone is looking to the future with somewhat mixed emotions.

READINGS: Philippians 4:4–9

John Keats, 'A Thing of Beauty', lines 1–19

Both of our readings speak of the passing of time, of what endures the passing of time.

For Saint Paul, things that are 'true … honourable … just … pure … pleasing or commendable' – these things endure, they are worth pausing and reflecting upon in the busyness of life.

For you, the long, hopefully hot summer holiday approaches; for some of you, there are new challenges and opportunities ahead, at college or university or in the world of work. For all of us, time, the future, stretches ahead. We all have a road to travel. And we all have to choose where to stop and reflect on this journey; what will make us pause and think, what lasts in this world where much is disposable.

As we each contemplate the journey ahead of us, let me tell you a story, a true story, which begins on a wild and stormy night.

In January 1992, a container ship en route from Hong Kong to America ran into trouble in the middle of the Pacific Ocean. With the ship rolling violently from side to side in heavy seas, several of the containers broke free from their moorings and tipped into the water. At least one was forced open, spilling its curious cargo of 29,000 plastic bath-time toys.

Pushed along by the wind and ocean currents, this flotilla of plastic yellow ducks – together with some red beavers, green frogs and blue turtles – began one of the world's greatest journeys; a journey that may now be nearing its end. More than thirteen years and several thousand miles later, scientists think that the toys have made their way up the western seaboard of North America, across the icy waters of the Arctic and are now bobbing their way down through the North Atlantic. Any day now, they could wash up on the shores of Britain.

It has been no idle pleasure cruise; these toys have been working during their trip. By monitoring where and when the drifting plastic creatures wash up on beaches, scientists have been able to study ocean currents in a way that's not been possible before. The ducks and their plastic friends have been helping experts trying to conserve fish stocks and trying to understand the effects of global warming.

The first recorded sighting of the toys was in November 1992 when six were washed up in Alaska, some 2,000 miles from where they were originally cast adrift. By alerting beachcombers and lighthouse-keepers, and publicising their quest in local papers, scientists managed to track down hundreds more over a 530-mile stretch of shore during the next year or so. The results were plugged into a computer to monitor the effect of surface currents on the ocean, and predictions began to be made about where they might turn up next. Some having been carried north, through the Bering Strait, they will have spilled into the Arctic Ocean sometime in the mid-1990s. From there, some are expected to have hitched a ride through the ice, and are due to hit our shores any time. The scientists in America are waiting for your call, should you come across a duck with the logo 'the first years' stamped on it, now faded from bright yellow to white. The red beavers are also a pale shadow of their former selves, although the turtles should still be blue and the frogs green.

I just love the idea of these toys liberated and roaming the seas, and being tracked by earnest scientists in white coats aided by a worldwide army of beachcombing volunteers. Toys which are restlessly seeking a place to stop, to be found and accounted for. Theirs is truly a grand adventure on a global scale.

I hope that each of you will have a life filled with grand adventures. I hope I have a few grand adventures ahead of me still. During some of these adventures, it will feel like we have little control over what happens; we are at the mercy of outside influences, the currents of life and circumstance. Others I hope we will create for ourselves, plan and make happen. All of these adventures will change us; some will make us stronger and more vibrant; others may take something out of us, perhaps leave us faded, a shadow of our former selves.

Who knows where we will end up, on what shore we will come to land? Who knows who will find us, or who will journey alongside us?

But this I do know: that some things are constant, in a world that keeps changing and in lives that move at a tremendous pace. There are things that are worth taking time to appreciate and develop in ourselves. So this I hope for each of you: that on the adventure of life that stretches ahead of you, you make space and time for some of the important and enduring things that Saint Paul and Keats talk about. That you take time:

- to stick up for the just and the true when the pressure is on to take the easy way out;

- to appreciate the natural beauty of our world, and to seek out the beauty each person carries within them, not relying on first impressions and outward appearances;

- to cultivate a purity of heart that makes integrity and honesty your way of life;

- to praise others where praise is due, and accept praise from others where it is deserved.

And this I pray for each of you: that in all the adventures of your life, you know something of the peace of God, a peace that is beyond our understanding, a peace that soothes and calms and lifts our spirits, a peace that guards our hearts and minds in Christ Jesus.

In the Grip of Fear

REV. EDITH McMILLAN

This poem was used along with Scripture references and personal experience as the basis of a high-school assembly on the topic of bullying and abuse, in conjunction with ideas expressed in 1 John 4:18 (RSV), 'Perfect love casts out fear'. The thoughts were expressed from personal experience of childhood difficulties to encourage the young folk to know that there are people around who will listen and support them when they face difficult times.

In the Grip of Fear

Fear – lose it, refuse it; get rid of its grasp,
Its vice-like hold stops you leaving the past.
It cannot control if you don't want it to,
Released from its grip, you can think and do.

Fear – tell those around you the things that distress,
With others to help you, the panic is less
able to hold you or keep you tight bound,
Released from such tension, new freedom is found.

Water, Wine and Chocolate Fountains

REV. KAREN HARBISON

Here are some elements of a worship service for you to dip into(!), focusing on the wedding at Cana and the overflowing, generous love of God which was revealed when Jesus changed water into wine.

READINGS: Isaiah 62:1–5, John 2:1–11

A chocolate fountain was placed on a table at the front of the church where everyone could see it. The chocolate fountain was all prepared and ready to go with chocolate previously melted, but was not switched on until the beginning of the time with the children. Pieces of fruit, fudge and marshmallows were prepared, put in bowls and covered with clingfilm. Cocktail sticks were ready too. The floor underneath the table was covered with a sheet to protect it.

Time with children

Ask the children if they like chocolate. Ask the children if they like parties. Tell the children that we are going to have a wee bit of a party today, and give them out party hats to wear. Tell the children that at our party we are all going to get some chocolate. Bring out bars of chocolate of various sizes, from single square to big bar, and each time ask the children if they think that will be enough to share around. (By this time, the children and everyone else can see and smell the chocolate in the fountain.) If the bar of chocolate is not enough to share around, ask the children if they have any suggestions about what we could do. Use the chocolate fountain.

Describe the fountain and how it is overflowing with chocolate. More than enough for everyone. Tell the story of Jesus going to a party, a wedding party, and how after a while the wine ran out. Jesus asked for big jars full of water to be brought to him, and he changed the water into wine so that everyone had more than enough. He did this to show God's love that was overflowing and for everyone, and he was glad when the people celebrated together.

In church today, the chocolate fountain is like a picture – it reminds us that God doesn't just give love that is like one square of chocolate, but he gives love that is overflowing and is more than enough for everyone, and we can celebrate that love.

Ask the children what would help them to remember – to taste the chocolate! Invite children to come up in small groups to dip fruit / sweets into chocolate – ask them how good it tastes.

Remind children that God's love is overflowing and is for us and for all.

Possible song to follow: 'God is good' (*CH4* – 178).

During offering, we had familiar folk tunes with wedding theme, like 'Mairi's Wedding', played on guitar and mandolin, and people tapped their feet, hummed the tunes or sang along.

Prayer of thanksgiving and intercession

It overflowed
wine in abundance, gallons and gallons of it.
You didn't just give enough to drink,
you didn't just give ordinary wine.
It was the best and more than enough for everyone.

It overflows
love in abundance, hugs and hugs of it.
You don't just give enough to get by,
you don't just give ordinary love.
It is the best and more than enough for everyone.

Loving Lord, we thank you for your abundant
    love,
love which lets us know we are not alone,
love which comforts our pain and suffering,
love which embraces our joy,
love which changes our lives and blesses us with life eternal.

Loving Lord, we pray for your abundant love,
your love for those who feel alone –
those who live alone,
those who are lonely,
those who have to cope with difficult situations and
    decisions on their own.

your love for those who are in pain and suffering –
those who are ill, who live with a daily struggle with pain,
those who are suffering because of disaster, poverty or
    violence,
those who are suffering the separation of bereavement, of
    distance or of dispute.

your love for those who are celebrating –
those who are celebrating marriage and a new stage in their
    relationships,
those who are celebrating the birth of a baby in their
    families,
those who are celebrating success and goals reached after
    time and effort.
your love for those who are in the midst of changes in their
    lives

and your love to change the lives of those who seek you at
   this time.

Loving Lord, may we share abundant love:
love for our family,
love for our friends,
love for the stranger,
love for our neighbours,
love to give comfort,
love to give encouragement,
love to give hope.
Lord Jesus
may our cups run over with your love
and may your love pour out through us
to bless the lives of all for whom we pray.
Amen.

Everyone sings the hymn 'Running over'.
   *Instead of leaving church immediately after the benediction, people
were invited to go to the front of the church and taste from the chocolate
fountain – reminding them of the abundant love of God there for them.
People stayed for ages dipping their fruit/sweets into the chocolate, tasting
the goodness of God, sharing with one another.*

Benediction
God has blessed you
with an abundance of love.
God's promise to the world
is filled to the brim
and overflowing.
Go into the world
to show God's overflowing love.
Go, and may the blessing of God
be with you now and for evermore.   Amen.

Section 7

Holy Week, Easter, Ascension and Pentecost

Holy Week Prayer

REV. LIZ GIBSON

This prayer links experiences described in the Bible to the lives we lead today and seeks to be as inclusive as possible.

God of glory and wonder,
we celebrate the gentle strength of your power.
You show us the power of a humble action –
Jesus riding on a donkey.
'Peace in heaven! Glory in highest heaven!'
So the crowds shouted as Jesus entered Jerusalem.
'Hosanna in the highest!'
At least on that day people recognised the power of your
      presence.
With them we sing your praises and acknowledge the hope
      you offer.
We pray that, as we remember that eventful week,
we may hold onto the hope
and understand the human failings which tried to kill it.

As we think about Satan entering into Judas,
forgive us for the times we have allowed Satan to work
      within us,
when we have known deep down that we are taking the
      wrong path
by choosing the easy option, going along with the crowd,

by wanting the wrong thing for the right reason,
or wanting the right thing for the wrong reason.

As we think about the disciples falling asleep,
forgive us for the times we have failed to get priorities right,
when we have worn ourselves out for the wrong reasons,
by rushing around doing things which aren't that important,
by worrying about the future instead of living in the present,
by forgetting the importance of frequent prayer.

As we think about Peter denying Jesus,
forgive us for the times we have denied him,
when we have trusted in our own strength instead of yours,
by seeing faith as separate from life rather than an integral
    part of it,
by focusing on the institution of the Church rather than the
    person of Jesus,
by valuing the world's opinion above our integrity.

Merciful God,
we know you understand the complexities of our very
    being,
we know you forgave your disciples, that Peter the denier
    was also Peter the rock,
that even Judas if he turned back to you would have been
    redeemed by your love.
In the silence now, we offer ourselves to you, asking your
    forgiveness ...
Accept the forgiveness God offers to you this day.

Generous God,
we thank you for the forgiveness you offer.
As we gratefully accept it, we ask too for the strength to
    make amends:
to reach out and say sorry to anyone we have hurt,

to own up and accept the consequences,
knowing that you will always be there for us,
to forgive others as we have been forgiven.
We bring all our prayers in Jesus' name.   Amen.

Love Can Give No More

REV. ANNE LITHGOW

*This meditation was written for a Holy Week service in East Linton.
Based on John 12:1–8, it has undergone several revisions over the years.
The measured pace of the meditation works in the context of a quiet,
contemplative service allowing space for thoughtful response. I hope that
it could be useful for ministers looking for material to help them at a
busy time of year.*

A home in Bethany,
A gathering one evening in the spring:

Martha, Mary, Lazarus, the hosts;
the guests are Jesus and his closest friends.

Twilight draws on to dark;
the lamps are lit,
the room is bathed in mellow glow
and comfortable laughter.

No stilted small talk here,
restraint or awkwardness.

Close friends need no formality,
and this was friendship quite unique.

Love Can Give No More

For Mary, Martha, Lazarus
owed to their honoured guest
the greatest debt conceivable.

Within that house, not long ago,
despair was turned to hope,
sorrow to joy, tears to delight,
when Jesus summoned Lazarus from death.

The gratitude, unspoken now,
is still profoundly felt,
expressed in loving hospitality.

There comes a lull when plates are cleared,
and guests lean back replete.

Into the stillness of the room comes Mary,
flask in hand;
breaks it and pours the richness over Jesus' feet.

Perhaps she meant
to scatter just a precious drop or two
upon his head?
Such was the custom, after all.

A little fragrance for an honoured guest.
Mark of respect, esteem.

That would have been enough.

Enough for etiquette,
but not enough for love.

The perfume flows,
the air is filled with heavy scent.

Mary inclines her head, lets her long tresses loose,
and gently wipes his feet.

There is no need for words. The deed says all:
Love has no limits.

He turns, catches her gaze, profoundly moved –

the man who lives for others' sake,
whose hands have touched the leper,
opened blind men's eyes,
embraced the little children,
broken bread.

Who of the many people he has met –
disciples, friends or bystanders –
has given him a gift
which asked for nothing in return?

Who else has let love's impulse rule,
without a thought of cost or consequence?

The silence in the room is palpable.

Mary has surely overstepped the mark,
gone far beyond the bounds of taste and decency.

Such intimacy –
hair let down in front of guests!
Such sinful waste!

Time seems to stop,
but then a tutting tongue, a disapproving frown,
a shaking head,

keeper of purse-strings for the twelve,
Judas Iscariot, breaks the spell.

He cannot comprehend the scene's significance,
the width and depth of love.

His ears are deafened by the chink of coins,
eyes blinkered with the balancing of books,
mind set on what convention would have done –

help for the poor, not out of love,
but as the duty of a pious soul.

Witness of love's extravagance
betrayed his friend, for cold, hard cash,
unable to see past a driven bargain
and a price for everything.

Too late it dawned on him
that love is only truly love
when it keeps nothing back.
But even Peter and the other ten
had failed to understand.

When Jesus spoke about his destiny of death,
Peter exclaimed:
'O, God forbid! No need to go as far as that.

Think of the folk who would not hear your word,
or feel your healing touch.'

'Satan, behind me now! At once!' was the retort.
'To sidestep Calvary
would be to set a limit on infinite love.'

Incomprehension lasted
through the Friday doom and dread,
and through the Sabbath emptiness,

until the first day of the week,
when Jesus stood among them once again –
proof tangible
that sprinkled drops are not enough.

The perfume must cascade upon the floor,
the blood flow down the splintered wood,
until the very last drop's spent
and love can give no more.

The Good Friday Worship Walk

REV. SUSAN ANDERSON

This Good Friday material had an element of surprise which encouraged people to come along the following year.

This worship service lends itself to movement through four separate areas, which could be four rooms or halls. Equally, four areas of the sanctuary could be prepared beforehand to embrace the concept.

All present had an order of service with hymns printed on it. Hymns are from *CH4*, and Scripture is read from the Good News Bible.

Travelling with Jesus

Area 1

Tonight, we shall go with Jesus from Jerusalem to the Mount of Olives and to Gethsemane, and then linger nearby before making our way back to Jerusalem. We travel in silence.

Start the service with all people gathered in the church.

READING: Matthew 26:17–30 (Jesus Eats the Passover Meal with His Disciples).

All sing hymn 376: ''Twas on that night'.

Injunction – 'Let us go to the Mount of Olives'.

Area 2

Choir sing hymn 371: 'Lay down your head'.

READING: Matthew 26:36–43 (Jesus Prays in Gethsemane), followed by a period of silence.

Prayer.

READING: Matthew 26:44–6 (as above).

All sing hymn 374: 'From heaven you came, helpless babe'.

Injunction – 'Get up, let us go'.

Area 3

Choir sing hymn 373: 'All is ready for the Feast', verses 1, 7, 8, 9.

READING: Matthew 26:47–56 (The Arrest of Jesus).

Pause for thought: 'What did the prophets say?' We particularly focus on Isaiah.

Injunction – 'We leave Jesus and run away'.

Area 4

READING: Matthew 26:57–68 (Jesus Before the Council).

Choir sing Church Anthem 24: 'God so loved the world'.

READING: Matthew 26:69–75 (Peter Denies Jesus), followed by a Prayer for Forgiveness.

Congregational hymn 482: 'Come let us to the Lord our God'.

Injunction – 'Come let us return to our God with clean hearts'.

Area 1

READING: Matthew 27:15–44 (Jesus Is Sentenced to Death; The Soldiers Mock Jesus; Jesus Is Crucified).

Congregational hymn 380: 'There is a green hill far away'.

READING: Matthew 27:45–50 (The Death of Jesus).

There should be just enough lighting for the person reading to be able to see.

The area is left in darkness.

Short silence followed by the Benediction.

All leave in silence.

A Good Friday Meditation

REV. ELSPETH DOUGALL

This Good Friday meditation was used at a united Good Friday service in Marchmont St Giles', Edinburgh, in 2001. The material worked well, as it involved people through the visual and through sung responses.

Chants, prayers, sung responses and times of silence may be used in between each meditation.

Pilate

READING: Matthew 27:11–26

ACTION: *A basin of water is brought forward and placed on the Communion table.*

MEDITATION: Pontius Pilate, prefect of Judea – an immensely powerful person with all the might of Rome at his disposal. Or so you would think, and yet in the accounts of Jesus' trial he comes over as singularly helpless. He was impressed by his prisoner, so calm and dignified, an innocent man. Clearly, he didn't want to condemn him to death – but, twist and turn as he might, he could not find a way to prevent it.

To a considerable extent, that was his own fault, because of the way he had trampled on Jewish religious sensibilities in the past. Where previous governors had dealt with the Jews with kid gloves, he had preferred the mailed fist. But his imperiousness had backfired. At various times, it had provoked a mass protest, riots, complaints to Rome; and more than once he had had to back down. These events had seriously undermined his position, with the result that now, faced with an angry mob baying for Jesus' blood, he simply did not have the moral authority to stand out against it.

I wonder what any of us would have done in his place? Responsible for keeping control of a city overcharged with religious fervour, knowing from bitter experience how volatile these Passover crowds were, would you have risked more riots? Would I have put my job on the line? Or would we too have decided it was better to sacrifice one man for the sake of peace and order?

Pilate washed his hands before the crowd, saying: 'I am innocent of this man's blood; see to it yourselves'.

The Soldiers

READING: John 19:17–24

ACTION: *A hammer and nails are brought forward and placed on the Communion table.*

MEDITATION: Every Good Friday, Edinburgh church members carry a cross to the top of Arthur's Seat and hold a service in a sheltered little amphitheatre just below the summit. One year, the wind was particularly strong, and the men on the hilltop had great difficulty keeping the cross upright. As they struggled with it, they shouted instructions to each other. They were so taken up with their own problem that they didn't realise that the service had begun. The sound of the reading and prayers, even of the singing, was whipped away by the wind. They heard none of it – but we could hear them, for their voices were blown straight down to us.

At first it seemed very inappropriate, and then it came to me that that was what it must have been like on Golgotha. While those who were personally involved were focused on suffering, on death, on loss, the soldiers were concentrating on a job of work – hammering in nails; shouting to each other as they raised the crosses up; settling down for the tedious wait until the crucified men died; passing the time by sharing out the clothes which were their perks; deliberately closing their minds to the pain and the indignity and the suffering just beside them. The job would be intolerable if you once allowed yourself to start thinking of the criminals as men with feelings, men with families.

And when they had crucified him, they divided his garments among them by casting lots; then they sat down and kept watch over him there.

The Friends

READING: John 19:25–30

ACTION: *A cross is brought forward and placed on the Communion table.*

MEDITATION: Meantime, where were Jesus' friends? His mother was there with her sister and Mary Magdalene and John. But what about the rest of the people who had shared his life for the last few years? Where were they?

Maybe some of them were among the crowd, trying to keep a low profile. That's what Peter had done earlier when Jesus was taken to the high priest's house, wanting to be loyal but defeated by fear. Maybe some of them were walking the streets of Jerusalem, or finding something to be busy with – doing anything other than face up to the reality of what was happening at Golgotha.

But the three Marys and John had that special kind of courage that could be there. They could face the fact that there was going to be a future when Mary would be a bereaved mother, and John would have to build a life without his beloved friend.

What nobody had realised yet was that the death that was taking place on the cross was going to transform the future. Pilate might perceive Jesus as an innocent who had got himself into a situation from which he could not be extricated. The soldiers might see him as another Jewish troublemaker. His friends might regard his death as waste and unbearable disappointment. But Jesus saw it as the necessary completion of the task he had committed himself to three years earlier, when he was baptised in the waters of the Jordan.

And what was that task? To pacify an angry God and persuade him to restore relationships with sinful men and women? By no means. The love of God had never faltered. But guilt and the fear that results from it has the effect of estranging sinful men and women from God, then as now. It is not God who needs to be changed, but we who need to be helped to find our way back to him.

All through his life, Jesus had been showing the way back; but it was only by enduring the cross that he could show how far love is prepared to go; it was only by allowing the power of evil to destroy his body that he could demonstrate the invincible power of love, which nothing can destroy.

Jesus said: 'It is finished'. And he bowed his head and gave up his spirit.

Chant:
Kyrie eleison (*CH4*, 776)

Prayer:
Generous God, we thank you for the love that reaches out to us, seeking us even when we turn away from you, offering us another chance when we have spoilt everything, dying that we might be forgiven, rising to bring new hope, new beginnings, new life. God, help us to accept your gifts and start anew.

Sung response:
O Lord, hear my prayer.
SILENCE

Today is your Dancing Day

REV. CARLEEN ROBERTSON

How did He feel, that third day, rousing from a different kind of sleep? Did He wake with a start, confused and unsure of where He was? Or was it a gentle coming to, a pleasant sensation, a feeling of peace?

Did He cry out with pleasure in feeling the stones under His feet, back on solid ground?

But it was dark in that cave. How He longed to see the sunlight again, breathe fresh air, fill His lungs with it until they were full to bursting.

This could not be right, shut in this dead man's resting place. It was a large stone covering the entrance, too big for an ordinary man to move. Did He smile as He made it roll away? Stones were no match for His power.

At last, the sun, newly born itself, flooded His soul, its warmth encompassed His cold body, its rays caused Him to shine.

It was not the dull white of a shroud He was wearing now, but the dazzling white of a festive robe. He stretched His arms out in delight, revelling in the space around Him.

Then He realised He was not alone. His heart sang out when He saw them approach: these women He had loved. He knew they loved Him too. They still loved Him, for they had come to make His dead body sweet.

His heart ached for a moment as they were filled with fear, tears pouring down their faces.

The stone had gone.

His precious body was not there.

What had happened to their Lord?

Their anguish was too much for Him. He could not bear to see them grieving, could not bear that look of pain in their eyes.

'Don't be afraid', He said to them. 'Death could not keep me. Yes, it has many powers, the power to paralyse minds with terror at the thought of it, the power to make the living be only half-alive, but the power to keep me no.

I have broken its hold forever, and, because it could not keep me, it shall not keep you.'

He didn't think they grasped what He was saying: who would? It was too much to take in, too much to get their heads round.

After all, they were still in shock at seeing Him, at standing so close to Him, hearing Him breathing – the one they thought would breathe no more.

He smiled at them.

Enough for now.

'Tell the others what you have seen,' He said, 'and then make for Galilee. There they will have the chance to see me too.'

Of course, He got there before them. Saw them coming, saw the puzzled looks on their faces, saw the doubters, the cynics, the ones who wouldn't, couldn't believe the words of a woman. He saw them all, and again love filled His heart.

His friends. His followers.

These were the ones who would take His love now to the world, to the four corners of the earth. And when the enormity of their task became too much for them, He would remind them that He has promised to be with them to the close of the age.

'I go before you', He said. 'Go before you into the unknown, into the difficult places, into the dark places, into the future. I go before you as I always have and as I always will.

Today is your dancing day.'

Easter in North India

REV. MARY WILSON

READINGS: 1 Corinthians 15:1–7, 12–20; John 20:19–29

Last Sunday was Easter Sunday, and all over the Western world it was celebrated with the singing of Easter hymns and the reading from John's Gospel of that first Easter morning. And after church, perhaps we went home to a special meal with family members home for the Easter holiday. In city churches, there were Easter breakfasts and the climbing of nearby hills at dawn, and dawn services and processions carrying the empty cross through the streets. And so, in so many ways, we celebrate Easter in the West.

But I want to tell you today about how we celebrated Easter in a tiny village called Pokhuria in northern India, where I worked as a nurse. We were a small Christian community, scattered over three or four villages of mud houses. We were among and surrounded by people of other faiths – Hindus, Muslims and animists. We felt ourselves to be identifiable, different and very close to each other. Christmas and Easter were our great days. The men who worked in the coal mines in the town would come home; there would be singing and drumming and church services, and we Christians would spend the whole day together eating our meals as picnics on the grass.

Easter was the greatest festival of all. It started on the Saturday with the noise of the men arriving home on the bus, some sitting on the roof, some clinging to the sides. Then, as it got dark, people started appearing on the pathways between the rice fields on their way to the graveyard. They carried storm lanterns or little oil lamps, and these were like stars in the dark. The graveyard was a clearing in a forest; the graves were mounds of earth smoothed out on the top with mud baked hard by the sun. The people had brought spades and water and so on, and all through the night they worked on the graves, building them up where they had been washed away by the rain. As they worked, the children played or slept, and the young people beat drums and sang.

By the time that the first light of Easter morning appeared in the sky, all the graves were ready. Flowers were strewn around, and it was all beautiful. The little lamps were extinguished, and the pastor stood up to start the Easter morning service. The forest became filled with the sound of singing: 'Jisui jiwet' beret' enae' – 'Jesus is risen and is alive'. It was no longer as if the graves round about us held dead bodies. It was as if our people were with us again – and it was not difficult to believe in the Resurrection.

But we are not in India in the tropical warmth and hot sunshine. We are sitting on the hard pews of Bonar Bridge Parish Church, and we are surrounded in our day-to-day living by people who don't believe in God at all. How are we to believe? Must Jesus appear to us as he did to Paul on the road to Damascus, or can we take the word of the women and the disciples for it? Whether we believe in the raising of the physical body or in a spiritual body or whatever – it doesn't matter how we hold it in our minds – but believe we must that something, that Easter morning, convinced the women that Jesus was alive. Otherwise, why would they have said it? They went to the tomb, after all, to anoint a dead body.

The excitement and joy experienced by the women and the disciples must have been tremendous – like the kind of thing that happened very occasionally during the war. A son reported dead would return home alive. That is the kind of experience these people must have had. It is the only explanation for the joy that sent them out into the streets to preach about their risen Lord and has kept people preaching ever since.

After the Resurrection and the Appearances, we become aware of a change in the way the disciples felt about Jesus. The Rabbi, the Teacher, with whom they walked and talked, ate and laughed and wept, had become the one to whom Thomas said: 'My Lord and my God!' and from then on they would call him 'the Lord'. But still he knew them as he did before. He still called them by their names – Mary, Peter, John – and still he understood them, their guilt and sorrow and shame as they ran away and left him.

This is the wonder of Easter, whether it be preached in India or Bonar Bridge. Jesus, who lived a human life on earth, and Jesus, our Risen Lord, who called the woman in the garden 'Mary', and even now calls us by name, are one.

Believe One Impossible Thing

REV. JULIE WOODS

From devastation to elation
From despair to hope
From anguish to joy
From pain to sheer pleasure …
He was alive!!
He was really, really, alive.

And they had seen him, touched him, heard him, known him …
and he had blessed them and wished them peace.

And suddenly it was all worth it: the fear, the terror, the
suffering, the isolation, the misunderstanding and the lack of
comprehension all faded into insignificance, for he had achieved
the impossible. He was back!!

The thoughts that filled their minds must have been jumbled
and confused. Believe one impossible thing every day, they say …
and here it is: Jesus, put to death in the most horrible way; Jesus
laid in a tomb, sealed in by a boulder that could not be moved
again; Jesus dead and buried, now alive again and bringing the
most outstanding news of all … God did all these things because
he loves us, because he wants us to be, as we were intended, united
with him for all eternity, in paradise!!

It is the most glorious, wonderful truth of all: God lives that
we too might live!

Ascension Dialogue

REV. SHIRLEY THOMAS

The Dialogue for Ascension was used at an evening service at Melville South Church, Montrose, in 2006. I believe that the dialogue is better than always a 'talking head'. The space between Ascension and Pentecost is a kind of no-man's-land, so this was written to reflect on Ascension and point on to the excitement of Pentecost.

Mary	Andrew! Is it true? Has He really gone for good?
Andrew	Yes. I saw Him go.
Mary	But how do you know that we won't see Him again? He has been coming and going for the last six weeks. You know that I saw Him myself when we had that big meeting up in Galilee.
Andrew	I know, Mary. I was there that time too. He came and spoke to about 500 of us. Then vanished just as He had that first time on the day He rose.
Mary	How was it different?
Andrew	Well, the other times He was there one minute and then gone the next. We didn't see Him go. But last Thursday we watched Him go. He took us up to the top of the Mount of Olives. Then He gave us instructions about what we were to do next. Then He rose off the ground, and this great cloud came down and we couldn't see Him any more.
Mary	What did you do?

Andrew	Nothing! We just stood there with our mouths open staring up into the cloud. I think we would have been there still if they hadn't spoken to us.
Mary	Who spoke? I thought it was just the eleven of you there?
Andrew	Well, suddenly there were these two men, dressed in white right there beside us. I suppose they were angels, but we didn't realise that at once. They asked us why we were staring into the sky. They said that Jesus had gone into heaven and that we would not see Him again until He comes again at the end of the world ...
Mary	So that's it, is it? What are we supposed to do now? It is really hard to have lost Him, found Him again and now lost Him. I feel very sad.
Andrew	No, Mary! You don't have to be sad. When He had that last supper with us, He promised that He would send His Holy Spirit to us. He will comfort us, give us power and keep reminding us of the Lord and all He ever taught us.
Mary	When is that going to happen? I don't feel very comforted and powerful. I'm still afraid the priests and the Romans will come to get us. I notice you still lock the door after you when we meet!!
Andrew	I know! Jesus didn't say when the Spirit would come. He just told us to stay in Jerusalem and wait.
Mary	It is hard to wait, especially when you don't know how long the wait will be. What are we to do while we wait?
Andrew	The best thing we can do is stick together and pray.
Mary	What do we pray about?
Andrew	The world!! The last command the Lord gave us was that we are to spread His message to the whole world.
Mary	How can we do that?
Andrew	I don't know. That's why we need to get praying.

Ascension Sermon

REV. EVELYN HOPE

Christ's liberating power

Paul wrote to the church in Galatia: 'Freedom is what we have –
Christ has set us free! Stand, then, as free people, and do not allow
yourselves to become slaves again' (Galatians 5:1, GNB).

It was the month of May, and I was well through my
year of serving as probationary assistant in King's Park Parish
Church, when I found myself helping with their Spring Fayre.
It was my lot, by my own choice, I may hasten to add, to be in a
small back room up behind the stage of the church hall, serving
teas and coffees to the stall convenors.

On this beautiful, warm May day, as, occasionally, I gazed out
the window to the sunny scene below, I saw youngsters jumping
with unrestricted abandon on the trampoline. As I listened to
their spirited, carefree laughter while others bobbed up and
down on the bouncy castle, that cooped-up feeling which we
all experience from time to time crept in on me. 'Fancy being
cooped up here on such a lovely day!' was the thought that
came to mind! I am sure you know what I mean by the effects
of being 'cooped up':

- tied to the house waiting for a tradesman who hasn't
  come when he said he would;

- confined to the office, or shop, or classroom when
  everyone else seems to be enjoying a good soak in the sun
  in the back garden;

- stuck in a caravan or hotel bedroom on a pouring wet day on holiday, when you are itching to get out and explore;

- or even when under doctor's orders you are forced to stay in bed indoors because of illness or injury;

- that feeling of frustration which accompanies deprivation of liberty!

Yet none of these things can emulate the experiences of those in the past who have been held hostages. As someone once said to me at the time one of the Middle East hostages was released: 'Imagine being blindfolded all that time!' I don't think any of us really could imagine such a thing. The deprivation of both sight and sound creates a tremendous sense of disorientation over and above the confinement and loss of liberty. The feeling of escape and freedom which that man must have had, I think, would have been beyond description.

This is the experience which Christ can bring to us!

This coming Thursday is the day that the Church has set apart to remember Jesus' final return to be with God, the Father. It has been called Ascension Day in the Church calendar. In the Gospel accounts after the crucifixion, we have recorded seven post-resurrection appearances of Jesus to his disciples. In Luke's Gospel this morning, we read: 'He departed from them and was taken up into heaven' (Luke 24:51, GNB).

Then, as we read also, Paul got caught up in this idea when he was writing to the Ephesians. Willie Barclay, explaining these thoughts of Paul, suggests that they go off at a tangent: 'He has used the word *ascended*, and that makes him [Paul] think of Jesus … Jesus *descended* into this world when he entered it as a man; Jesus *ascended* from this world when he left it to return to his glory … the Christ of glory', Barclay says, 'is the same as the Jesus who trod this earth …'.

But Jesus, he goes on, 'did not ascend up on high to leave the world'; he did so 'to fill the world with his presence. When Jesus was here on earth in human form, he could only be in one place at one time ... returned to glory, he was set free from the limitations of the body and was able then to be everywhere in all the world through his Spirit' (*The New Daily Study Bible: The Letters to the Galatians and Ephesians* (Edinburgh: Saint Andrew Press, 2002), pp. 165–6).

We might say he became a free spirit, no longer tied to, or bound by, our earthly life's limitations.

A new stained-glass window, which was installed in King's Park Church while I was there, was designed by a ten-year-old girl and symbolises this idea very well. In the foreground are two empty crosses. Asked 'Why two crosses?', this ten-year-old, with great insight, replied: 'To show that Jesus is everywhere!' And indeed, she has inscribed on one of the crosses: 'Jesus is', and on the other alongside ... the word 'everywhere'!

So, his Spirit came to the disciples at Pentecost, which the whole Church will be celebrating shortly. His Spirit is now able to roam freely, seeking out the hearts and minds of people quite independently of nationality, or race, or geography; his Spirit is freed to reach out and touch and respond to all who are in need and cry out for his love and comfort, irrespective of when in time or where in space that cry comes to him.

But what exactly does Christ's return to that higher, other world, exalted dimension of God's Kingdom, mean for us worshipping here in South Shawlands this morning? What has that got to do with us now?

Well, I think it has liberated us also in at least three ways.

One way in which Christ has set us free is that we need no longer be burdened and weighed down with fears and anxieties and guilt. 'Come to me,' he invites us, 'all who are over-burdened and heavy laden and I will give you rest.' He recommends we should stop getting all het up about what might happen tomorrow because there is enough to think about and concentrate upon in just living our lives today. Now, that is something many of us are not very good at in Western society in this day and age – that is, if medical statistics on 'stress-related illnesses' are anything to go by; and the management of stress has become big business in the workplace in Europe and the USA in recent times. It has even been taken on board as an issue in the Church of Scotland because some of our ministers have come down with what has come to be termed 'burn-out'.

What it boils down to in the end really is – take time out; do something different; find a way to 'unwind'. Jesus knew about that. How many times in the Gospels do we read about him seeking a quiet place to rest and pray? Think about the demands made upon him.

Yet he managed to escape to spend time with God 'far from the madding crowd', and he offers us the same opportunity to take our worries to him. Jesus gives us the reassurance that, if we pray about whatever the problem is, and then put the worry behind us – if we are able to do that, then a great weight will be taken from our shoulders. He will free us from all fears and our feelings of guilt.

The second way in which I think he liberates us is by freeing our minds. He opens up our access to God, for he did teach a very new thing. He taught his disciples to address God as 'Our Father' – Abba – Dad – the term for a truly close relationship.

Jesus challenges our thinking and our decision-making all the time. Remember that he frequently stood the rabbinic law on its head.

- He challenges us when we drum up excuses as we react inappropriately for a Christian in certain situations;
- He challenges us about the priorities we set for ourselves;
- He causes us to question our opinions and our prejudices.

Few of us like to think we hold racist views, yet the media continues to uncover injustices of a racial dimension in Britain. When these issues are raised – like immigration and asylum-seekers – some even coming to live in our own community, our Christian position is challenged. How does it stand up to scrutiny?

Christ also keeps on challenging us out of the ruts we persist in crawling into because of the feeling of security they offer. I am not suggesting we can all just tear up our roots and abandon our comfort zones; but it makes you think, doesn't it? Sometimes we clutter up our lives with preconceived ideas, and we preciously hold onto traditions, which, in many instances, have become like millstones around our necks. Churches of all denominations around Scotland are, even now, in a state of crisis and fighting for survival. We need to reopen our minds to those things that really matter. We need to listen to that verse in John's Gospel – John 8:32 (GNB) – which says: 'Then you will know the truth, and the truth will set you free'. And we do this by listening to the Holy Spirit of our Risen Lord – the voice of God himself, and so we are set free of the shackles and constraints of narrow-mindedness and blind repetition.

A third way in which the exalted Christ liberates us is that he frees us to serve and to witness for him.

At about the age of 90, Catherine Bramwell Booth, granddaughter of William Booth, founder of the Salvation Army, admitted in an interview: 'I think the public work was the most difficult. I shrank from it. I felt my own nature was opposed to it. All the things I loved were private things, and I used to pray, "O Lord, you know I'm no good at public work"' – and yet she, at the age of 100, was able eventually to face an audience of millions in a TV interview – and was a real hit at that!

By his liberating Spirit, Christ sweeps away our inhibitions and fears of inadequacy, and in him we find power to speak out and to witness.

So, then, on this Sunday immediately before Ascension Day, it is good to remember Jesus finally returned to be with the Father. We also, in the power of the Spirit, are freed to serve; freed to think; and freed of all anxiety and care.

Sowing in the Field of the Spirit

REV. CAROLINE TAYLOR

If the Spirit is the source of our life, let the Spirit also direct our course. (Galatians 5:25, NEB)

She had just moved into a new house. Well, perhaps it would be more accurate to say that she had just moved into a new garden. For it was the ground surrounding the house that had drawn her to put in a bid. She was no housewife, nor did she aspire to be.

Among the things she enjoyed most in life were the feel of soil, the growth of seedlings, the abundance of butterflies, the vibrant colours of tulips, roses, petunias and chrysanthemums.

She was a gardener. Her garden was the most important thing in her life, she would have told you.

She was not a stupid woman. She had a good head on her shoulders, was not one given to introspection.

So, she was not aware of the other garden she had planted. What we might call the spiritual garden.

There too, the products of her steady labour took root, blossomed and produced fruit.

There was self-control.

When she woke one morning to find that someone had yet again stuffed beer cans into the front hedge.

There was gentleness.

In the way that she spoke to the birds as if they were her best friends.

There was fidelity.

For it would not have occurred to her to go away in the summer when hanging baskets require daily watering.

There was goodness.

In her unselfish handing out of strawberries, lettuces and plums to the neighbours.

There was kindness.

In her willingness to let the little girl from across the road ply her with questions for want of a playmate of her own age.

There was patience.

As she waited for growth, and the right time to harvest.

There was peace.

Anyone in her company discovered that. She listened with the same sort of attentiveness that she gave an ailing plant. She didn't hurry you. She didn't judge you. She didn't apportion blame or hand out a ticket for a guilt trip.

There was joy.

In the faces of the residents of the nursing home to whom she took bunches of daffodils in the spring and bunches of sweet peas in the summer.

There was love.

Above all, there was love. Not just for her garden, which she would have called her chief love.

But also for the lonely little girl, the neighbours with their stressful lifestyle, the frail elderly folk, even for the vandals who couldn't see that there was beauty in her garden which ought to remain unspoiled.

As Paul inspires us (based on Galatians 6:7–10):

> Make no mistake about this: God is not to be fooled; a person reaps what she sows if she sows in the field of the Spirit, the Spirit will bring her a harvest of eternal life. So let us never tire of doing good, for if we do not slacken our efforts we shall in due time reap our harvest. Therefore, as opportunity offers, let us work for the good of all, especially members of the household of this faith.

Section 8
Advent and Christmas

A Blue Christmas Prayer

REV. SHEILA CRAGGS

This prayer and words of hope were part of a service for those people who felt unable to fully enter into the spirit of Christmas for one reason or another. It followed the lighting of candles, by anyone who wished to remember a loved one, coming forward to the tables set up at various points in the church.

Father, in the spirit of this season, let us now confidently pray for ourselves as we participate in whatever we can this Christmas.

Father, we pray for our families and friends that they may continue to help and support us. We remember those we have loved and have lost, who are no longer here with us but resting in your beloved arms. We remember all kinds of losses, of jobs and homes, of friends and workmates.

Father, we pray that all may know love and peace and happiness in you.

Father, you are a God of all seasons and senses. Grant us the sense of your timing to submit gracefully and rejoice quietly in the turn of the seasons.

In this season of short days and long nights, of grey and white and cold, teach us the lessons of endings; children growing, friends leaving, loved ones dying, grieving over, grudges over, blaming over, excuses over. Father, grant us a sense of your timing.

(Time for silent prayer)

In this season of short days and long nights, of grey and white and cold, teach us the lessons of beginnings; that such waiting and endings may be the starting place, a planting of seeds which bring to birth what is ready to be born – something right and just and different, a new song, a deeper relationship, a fuller love – in the fullness of your time. Father, grant us the sense of your timing.

(*Time for silent prayer*)

As these candles glow, Father, help us in our remembering to keep the flame alight in the way we move on and live our lives. Keep us safe in your love, and grant us your peace this night and always.   Amen.

Words of Hope

Each of us gathers treasures of memories and experiences, of teachings and principles as we age and mature. So we accumulate a rich treasure. Christmas seems to be an especially poignant time for drawing out these memories that reach as far back as childhood.

Songs, sights and traditions all have rich emotions attached that give meaning to what we do this season. The ancient story that Luke tells about the birth of Jesus is one of those treasures we hear and store away.

For all of us, certain people make up the memory treasures in our life. Tonight, we have gathered here to worship and remember those people who are no longer with us because of death, divorce, separation or other loss. We have remembered those who are sad and lonely. In our worship, we have lifted our voices in praise and given thanks, and remembered our loved ones. Jesus told his disciples what the Kingdom of God is like. And then he said that whoever remembers these teachings is like the master of the house who draws out treasures old and new.

So, that is what we have done tonight. During our worship, we have drawn out the treasured memories, reflected on the lives that were shared with us, and that gave us so much. And in so doing, we have transformed our past memories into rich treasures that give meaning and delight in remembering and telling stories about them – especially at Christmas.

Tonight, we can have hope that, in the coming of God's Son once again at Christmas, we will remember but begin again our journey, walking hand in hand with Jesus Christ until we reach the Kingdom where we will all be reunited and at peace.

May God grant you hope, love, peace and joy this Christmas and throughout the coming year.

Art for Advent

REV. SANDRA BLACK

The congregation in Toryglen worked with Carol Marples from 'Soul Marks' through the church year, using art in our worship for the major festivals. This is an outline of the series of services we did for Advent 2005. The group that met with Carol to think about what we should do for Advent expressed the feeling that celebrating the Sundays of Advent is becoming more important for us as Christians as Christmas becomes increasingly secular and commercial.

We spent a Saturday in late November preparing materials for each of the Advent services. Each week, there was something new to see.

For the first Sunday in Advent, we put up the words Hope, Peace, Joy and Love. Each word was written on black paper with gold paint. All the words were covered with black paper, and one word was revealed each week. A candle was lit each Sunday, the word uncovered and the theme introduced.

Week 1

THEME: Hope in darkness

READING: Isaiah 64:1–9

The members of the congregation were each given a cut-out candle symbol on yellow paper as they came into church. They were invited to write on the candle something that they hoped for in their own lives or something that they hoped for the world.

The candles were collected and displayed so that they were seen when the congregation entered the church the following Sunday. We strung the candles up on fishing wire and hung them across the width of the church; but other ways of displaying them would suit different buildings.

Week 2

THEME: Peace in God's presence

READING: Isaiah 40:1–11 and Mark 1:1–8

The members of the congregation were each given a dove folded from white paper as they came into church.

As we thought about the theme, the congregation was invited to think of what was needed to make the world a more peaceful place and about what God's peace meant to each of them. We sat in silence for a short while. People were invited to write their thoughts on the doves' wings if they wished. The doves were collected during the service and displayed like the candles for worship the following week.

Week 3

THEME: Joy in going God's way

READING: Luke 1:24–55

This was our Communion Sunday, and the symbol we used this week was God's invitation to us. A pre-printed invitation was given to each person as they came into church. Their name was written on it for them by one of the welcome team. During the service, everyone was invited to reflect on how God invites every one of us to his presence; and we played music during this reflective time. The invitations were collected and displayed for the following Sunday.

Week 4

THEME: Love came down at Christmas

READING: Luke 2:1–7

This was an All-Age service, and the children were present throughout, so the theme fitted in with the children's telling of Jesus' birth at Bethlehem.

Everyone was given a star cut out of silver card on entering the church.

During the service, the adults and older children were invited to write on each of the five points of the star:

- The name of someone you care for (we always use first names only to protect privacy when we use individuals' names)

- The name of a place where you would like to see peace

- Something that makes you happy

- Something you would like to change

- The name of someone you want to pray for.

The younger children were given colouring pencils to decorate their stars.

As before, the stars were gathered in and used to decorate the church for the Christmas Eve and Christmas Day services.

This was a noisy activity where people chatted about what they were doing, but it could easily be used quietly and contemplatively.

Dark Enough to
See the Stars

REV. MAUREEN LEITCH

This article of hope and healing was written as a result of my realisation that Christmas wasn't a joyful time for everyone. I wanted to offer a different approach, and so this was offered as a Sunday afternoon service. It worked well because it acknowledged the pain that some feel as Christmas approaches and allowed them the 'space' to be sad or tearful or reminiscent.

The ancient Persians have a saying: 'When it is dark enough, you can see the stars'.

Today is the first Sunday in Advent – the period of waiting-time leading up to Christmas. As you can see, the church is decorated especially for this period. Yet, the colour the Church chooses for this time is not red for the Santa suit, or green for the tree, or white for the snowy tinsel … but purple.

Purple … the sombre colour of mourning, waiting and reflection. For we believe that we may not be able to see the child unless we have first lived through the dark hours.

Hours of waiting and reflection.

And, although you probably don't feel that you are favoured because you have suffered loss, there is a sense in which you just may be in a better position than many to see the child in the manger.

For when things are darkest, you can see the stars.

Now, that is not a call to be cheerful in the face of the storm. Nor is it a call to cheer up because the problem is just in your head. It is a realistic acceptance of all that buffets life. It is a call to the Christian hope that God will act when we cannot. He knows our sorrows and our difficulties and will help … if we let him. He will bring victory to all who believe. Even death does not thwart him. It thwarts us … but God's resurrecting power brings life out of death. This is a difficult time for those who have suffered loss. But it is important that we take time in Advent to acknowledge our loss.

The Gospel text assigned for today does not speak of the baby at all (Luke 21:25–36). Instead, it talks of times of great destruction and darkness. Jesus said that, when things are dark, you will see the triumphant Christ coming in glory.

You may wonder what any of this has to do with Christmas. But it is just one of Jesus' teachings on hope. It is a call to hope for those facing hard times. And I guess that includes most of us, for one reason or another. Jesus tells us that when there is nothing you can do – nothing – then God will act on your behalf. When you are at the end of your tether – when you have no power to fight circumstances that are engulfing you, then it is time to lift your head.

And I invite you all to make the journey to the manger in your sorrow. Come to the child who brought love into the world. For those whose world is darkest have the best chance of seeing him.

Who will see him? The wretched, the suffering, the humble shepherds, three men looking for a king they could not find on their travels.

And who will be blest? The pure in spirit, the pure in heart, those who mourn. Advent is a dark time. How dark?

Dark enough to see the stars.

It is in these stars that we have our hope and also the beginning of our healing.

Let us take time now to remember those who are dear to us but are no longer with us physically. Let us bring our stone to the cross – there to leave it with God. If you wish, you may light a candle in memory of a loved one. That candle will be lit again on Christmas Eve to bring light to the sanctuary as we move into Christmas Day. As we come to celebrate the birth of our Saviour.

Christmas Colours

REV. DOROTHY ANDERSON

This is a summary of a Christmas service, which I have done more than once in different locations. I have had it performed as a Nativity play, with children having speaking parts (the older ones told the Noah story in rhyme on one occasion). Or with narrators and actors; but I have also narrated it myself and used volunteers from the congregation, adults as well as children, to form a tableau.

The idea is to tell the Christmas story using the colours of the rainbow. Add hymns/songs, prayers and so on appropriate to your setting.

Begin with Genesis 7:1–10, 21–3; 9:12–17.

Talk about the rainbow – seven colours (I had suitably coloured ribbons inside all hymnbooks and asked people to find and wave them, creating a rainbow across the church). Ask: Which colour do you associate with Christmas?

The seven colours are then explained like this – interspersed with whatever readings and music you think right.

Mary

If we think about Mary, mother of Jesus, we often think of her wearing BLUE.

In truth, we don't know what colour she wore, but she is shown in blue because blue is the colour of truth and purity and heavenly love. And of holiness in God's service.

So, it reminds us how much Mary was loved by God and how loyal she was to him.

But it was also the colour of the sky, which was thought to be the place that separated God from his people. So, blue was the colour of the boundary between heaven and earth – and Mary was the person who was seen as the boundary/link between heaven and earth – the human being who gave birth to God.

As such, she was entitled to be seen in blue – a go-between for God and humans.

Blue also represents physical protection – as a mother, it was her task to protect the baby she carried and gave birth to.

Joseph and the innkeeper

Which people in our Christmas story wear ORANGE and YELLOW?

Not often do we see Joseph wearing orange; but I suggest that he should.

Orange is the colour for strength and endurance. It also symbolises creativity – and Joseph was a carpenter – and new homes. When Jesus was born, Joseph was the one who had to give him a new home on earth. Not just one either – first they had to flee to Egypt, and later they returned to Nazareth.

More importantly, orange is the colour that reminds us of change. Think of the sky just as day fades and the darkness approaches – and you'll think of orange sunsets. So, it is a sign of change and the ability to adapt. And there's no doubt that Joseph's life changed quite dramatically from the moment he heard about Mary's baby right through.

So, Joseph is in orange.

Yellow, then, is for the innkeeper. Partly because of the lantern he carried to show the way to the stable; but mainly because it stands for faithfulness and energy and insight. Something told the innkeeper that night not just to turn the weary travellers away but also to offer them his stable. Yellow is also the colour associated with God's love for us – the love that was born in that stable, in the pale yellow light of the innkeeper's lamp.

Shepherds

I think most of you will have worked out what colour suits the shepherds. It's GREEN, of course.

Green represents springtime and growth and new life. It is a sign of hope and of nature and eternal life. Think of flowers that grow and flower and die back – but grow again in the spring.

It is a sign of peace and tranquillity – just as in Psalm 23 we hear that the Lord is a shepherd who makes us lie down in green pastures. For rest and peace.

And it was out in the fields, among the plants and animals, that the shepherds heard the news of the birth of Jesus, the sign of hope for them and for the whole world. The sign of eternal life.

Wise men

Recap. Blue, Orange, Yellow, Green. Which leaves what? RED, INDIGO, VIOLET.

Deal with all of them at once. These are the rich, royal colours suitable for the wise men.

All purple colours are signs of riches. They come from expensive plant dyes, which only the wealthy could afford to buy. So, in the Bible, purple is used for the decorations in the Temple and for kings.

Indigo in particular was very costly, but it was long-lasting and so stood for power and importance. But it is also the colour of meditation and insight – we know that the kings studied long and hard and that in the baby Jesus they recognised the Saviour.

Purple is also a sign of sadness and suffering – and, as we know, the gifts that the kings brought with them were signs that Jesus would suffer. So, it is right that the kings wear both indigo and violet.

Red is the colour of strength and courage but also of life and love. And so, as the king wears it, it is a sign of the love he had for the Christ child, as well as the love he has for each of us.

Light

So, what colour is Christmas?

It is every colour – the whole spectrum.

But it is also no colour – it is white. White light can be split into the seven rainbow colours – from brightest red to darkest purple.

Jesus is that light – the white light which came into the world to overcome the world's darkness. He is the light that still shines, for you and me and everyone, from the poorest of shepherds to the richest of kings. For people of this country and every country, people of every age and colour and class.

So, Christmas is rainbow-coloured. R O Y G B I V, as seen in the rainbow by Noah so many thousand years ago – a sign of God's promise then and now.

It is rainbow-coloured – for black and white, yellow and brown, male and female, rich and poor.

And it is white. Those colours merged 2,000 years ago in the birth of a baby in Bethlehem, Jesus – the light of the world.

The Word is Out

REV. TINA KEMP

This has been used at Christmas Eve services over the years, in both small-group and larger worship settings. I believe that people can identify with the personalisation of specific biblical passages, and know that they enjoy imagining how particular characters felt.

The Word is out.
> It comes in the beat of angels' wings. In ancient promises.
> In the sigh of innocence. In the wisdom of age.

The Word is out.
> It speaks in the despair of prophets. In the silence of sealed
> lips.
> In a carpenter's disgrace. In the nudges of gossips.

The Word is out.
> It shakes shepherds with its clarity. Shocks kings with its
> bluntness.
> Summons star men in its echo.
> And soothes beasts with its breathing.

The Word is out.
> The silent word of God. Sucks in its earthly breath
> And cries life on this holy night. Disturbing the stillness.
> Defying the calm. Rocking in uneasy peace.

The Word is out.
> Crying flesh and blood. Wriggling bones and skin.
> Speaking the unspoken. Asking, seeking love.

Once and for all. The Word is out.

Section 9

Prayers

Two Introits

REV. MARY HENDERSON

These introits arose from a challenge set by my organist in May 2001. The challenge was to write words for some new introits, which he would put to music and the choir would sing during the month of June, when there was no anthem. Copies of the music may be had from me.

Introit 1

Spinner of Substance,
Draw out our beauty;
Twist in our strength;
Wind us into one.

Weaver of Words,
Straighten our warp;
Disentangle our threads;
Create our pattern.

Tailor of Truth,
Take the measure of us;
Stitch up our wounds;
Clothe us in splendour.

Introit 2

Rhythm of heartbeat, and pulsing of life;
Shielding of husband, and nurture of wife;
Fashioning worlds, bringing peace out of strife;
Work on us still, Creator.

Teller of tales and disturber of calm;
Victor and victim, both Shepherd and Lamb;
Calling disciples, who came (with a qualm);
Beckon us on, Lord Jesus.

Closer than heartbeat, and softer than sigh;
Here in our living, and there when we die;
Source of our laughter, and depth of our cry;
Dance with us, Holy Spirit.

Assembly Week Prayers 2007

THE VERY REV. SHEILAGH KESTING

Thursday 24 May

Opening responses

Moderator	It is God who created us,
ALL	**male and female he created us.**
Moderator	It is Christ who has reconciled us to God And given to us a ministry of reconciliation.
Men	**There is no longer Jew or Greek**
Women	**There is no longer slave or free**
ALL	**There is no longer male or female for we are all one in Christ Jesus.**
Moderator	It is the Spirit that prays within us
ALL	**bearing witness that we are children of God.**
Moderator	The Lord be with you
ALL	**And also with you.**

Prayer of adoration and confession

As a mother comforts her child,
    so you comfort us, O God,

you nourish us and encourage us with love
and tend our wounded feelings with gentleness.
You smile with us when we push the boundaries
and venture into new places
learning by our mistakes and maturing
in understanding and in sensitivity.
You weep for us when we turn our backs on you,
when we hurt others by our thoughtlessness or by wilful
intent,
when we do not love one another as you love us
nor forgive others as we are forgiven.
You are patient with us,
willing our return to you,
impatient to see us reconciled to one another and to you.

Lord, have mercy
Christ, have mercy
Lord, have mercy.
Take from us the burdens of sorrow and guilt that we
need carry no longer
and set us free once more to serve you as we ought
with our mouths filled with praise
our hearts with gladness
and our souls with peace.
This we ask in Jesus' name.
Amen.

Prayers of thanksgiving and intercession

Let us give thanks for the church throughout all ages
for the ministry of all who are baptised
a ministry of proclamation, of care, of hospitality.
We give thanks for men and women who are called to serve
as elders, deacons and ministers of Word and Sacraments,
in chaplaincy or in parish
for their costly walking with those who are wounded by
the brutalities of life

and who seek comfort and assurance for the next stage of
their journey.
We give thanks for the ministry of the Guild,
as it increases awareness and sensitivity,
encouraging informed solidarity and selfless
service
among those who are most vulnerable both near and
far.
We give thanks that you have called **us,** each one, into the
company
of those who have put their trust in Christ and who seek to
obey his will.
Hear us as we pray for the Church in all places
that its ministry may be exercised in humility and with
courage
reflecting the ministry of Christ as the one who came to
serve
and bringing to blossom the loving potential within all
people.
We pray for those who in faith continue to wrestle with the
Church
who recall it to its purpose when it has made its own laws
more important than your Gospel
that they may not lose heart.
We pray for all who exercise ministry:
where their faith has become jaded by the ambiguities of
life
may they be sustained by the prayers and love of
those around them;
where they are burdened by a sense of their own
shortcomings
may they be aware of being valued as the people they
are;
where they are exhausted by the demands of their ministry
may they be refreshed for a new day.

We pray that through the ministry of the Church in this land
   the common life of the people may be enriched,
   and the decisions of those in authority may be
      strengthened for goodness and truth.
We pray for those who seek our ministry;
   those who suffer in body or in mind;
   the anxious and the sad,
   those whose trust has been abused
   those who find it hard to know they are lovable.
We pray especially today for those who have HIV and AIDS
   and for those who minister among them
   in churches, projects and clinics that seek an end to
      stigmatisation
   and ensure a high quality of life for those affected.
      May they feel the warmth of your embrace.
And hear us as we commit ourselves and the business of
   this day to your service
   that all we say and do may be pleasing in your sight
   and worthy of the ministry you have given us.
Our Father ... Amen.

Friday 25 May pm

Prayer of adoration and confession

In your grace you have created the universe and all that is in it
   you have allowed the earth to evolve
   you have watered it
   and provided nourishment for its creatures.
You have set within it a people, male and female,
   to reflect your image
   to articulate the praise of creation
   to treasure the gifts you have given
   to explore the possibilities of goodness that lie hidden
   beneath the surface of ignorance and hurt.

225

Forgive us when we ignore the promptings of your spirit, God
within us,
    when we fail to look for signs of your goodness in others.
    Forgive us when we forget how vulnerable you became in
    Jesus Christ,
    God with us,
    when we set ourselves unrealistic standards of goodness.
Forgive us when we stand between you and those you
love
    as figures of judgement rather than mercy
    of self-righteousness rather than understanding.

    Lord, have mercy,
    Christ, have mercy.
    Lord, have mercy.
Draw us back into the heart of your embrace
    that we might feel again your nearness to us
    when we are at our most vulnerable,
    when we are open to questions and to
        self-doubt
    so that we may be able to embrace others
    and find wholeness through serving them
    in the strength of your Holy Spirit within and among us.
    Amen.

Prayers of thanksgiving and intercession

We give thanks for the cloud of witnesses
    that have kept hope alive in all generations.
    for those who have gone before us and been a source of
        inspiration to us
    for our contemporaries who witness to your love on the
        margins of society
    for those who will keep that flame of hope alive in
        generations to come,

those whom we have touched as lives have
crossed
and opportunities have been grasped.
We give thanks for the places of healing in all lands,
for people who bring hope to the poorest communities
of our world
for those who give voice to the voiceless
and dignity to those who have nothing.
for those who seek justice for all people
and careful use of the earth's resources.
We give thanks for those who minister to the needs of the
sick and the dying,
who offer a welcome to those who seek refuge from
violence and despair
who show by their example the depth of your care.
As we come towards the end of this General Assembly,
we give thanks for the people throughout the Church
of Scotland
who give faithful witness to you from day to day
in their homes and in their places of work,
in business and in leisure
for the stories we have heard in the course of our
business
of places where hope is reborn and community life is
supported,
for the witness offered by those gathered here this
evening
who stand on the threshold of a new period of their
lives;
for those who are setting out and for those who are
finishing.
We ask a blessing on those who yearn
for love and dignity
and the healing of body, mind or spirit
that they might find inspiration and peace
through those who are called to care.

And as we prepare to bring this General Assembly to a closure
>we pray that we may go from here
>with the light of your love in our eyes
>and the fire of your love in our hearts.
Go with his Grace as he takes his leave of us
>having fulfilled his commission
>and with those who have supported him in the carrying
>>out of his duties
>in this past week.
Guide and strengthen us in mission and service to the world
>wherever we find ourselves.
Keep us looking outwards to the world,
>open to the needs of others;
>and use us in all our frailties
>as part of that vast cloud of witnesses in heaven and on
>>earth
>with whom we continue to pray in the words we were
>>taught to say together:
Our Father ... Amen.

Dismissal and blessing

Let there be no day on which you say
>there is no-one to give me a hand.
Let there be no day on which you say
>there is no-one to walk with me.
Let there be no day on which you say
>there is no hope.
Go in peace to love and serve the Lord.
And now may the grace, mercy and peace
of God the Father, the Son and the Holy Spirit
be with you all, both now and always.   **Amen.**

Prayer of Thanksgiving

REV. WENDY DRAKE

Within this book is a variety of prayers. Here, Wendy shares with us the fact that her prayer of thanksgiving is written in a more female mode than she would normally write, but feels that it is appropriate for the purpose of this book.

O Spirit of the living God,
>	we give you thanks for your eternal presence with us.
Of old, we have heard stories of your faithfulness.
Of our present, we are recipients of your loving-kindness.
For the future, we depend on you to guide our every
>	footstep.
Today, we give you thanks particularly for those who have gone
>	before us in the faith,
>>		giving us inspiration, encouragement
>>		and lively examples of the possible variety of Christian
>>>			work and witness.
We are thankful for the women and men who fought to have
>	the place of women within the Church
>>		a mission beyond making the tea and supporting the
>>>			men;
for the people who have felt called to preach the Gospel and
>	spread the good news of Jesus
>>		beyond their immediate circles of families and friends.
We thank you for women and men who have been called by
>	you to expand their education and experience,

and bring to the Church their faith enhanced by their
unique experience of life.
We are grateful for all these people, *of* every age and *in* every
age, of whatever gender,
who have encouraged everyone in their vocation.
Our prayers, too, are for those who have not recognised, or find
it difficult to recognise, that you, O Lord,
have called human beings to minister within your Son's
Church.
Each of us and all of us have different gifts and abilities;
Enable us, Lord, to give them to you gladly, as you have
given us.
In each day and every generation, you have given us all the task
of sharing the good news of Jesus' love.
Help us, Lord, not to be bound by the conventions of any era
which could lead to the holding back of love.
May we be challenged by the eternal now
on which you are God
and in which that love must be shared,
in Jesus' name through whom we ask all our
prayers.   AMEN.

Prayer of Intercession

REV. SHEILA CRAGGS

- Loving heavenly Father, we come into your presence once again to offer our love and our thanks for being with us this morning. You offer us so much, and we thank you especially for the gift of your beloved Son, Jesus Christ.

- Generous God, sometimes we don't even notice your gifts. They're there all round us, just waiting for us to pick them up and use them, but we don't see them. And it can be like that with your answers to our prayers. Sometimes we think you're mute, but actually we have failed to spot your response.

- Generous God, give us discernment and wisdom and the motivation to observe and receive and use all your many gifts. Above all, teach us in our inner being just what it means to receive you as the Bread of Life; that we may begin to experience eternal life right here and now, and prepare to walk straight through into your kingdom after our death.

- Gracious Father, through your creation you have given us the gift of the Church so that Christ's presence with us may have a focus. But we grumble and find fault continually about the Church's imperfections because we fail to see it as a gift from you and we fail to notice that we, the members, are part of that gift. Open our eyes, that we may see not the imperfections but the glory of the gift, and enable us all to work to enhance that glory.

- Father, you are a just God. You have given us a world full of beauty with natural resources to accommodate our every need. Give all people the gifts of generosity and love, that your resources may be properly used and distributed for the good of all and for your glory. May any facing a ruined harvest be helped by caring people throughout the rest of the world, and may any facing a life marred by violence be assured of your peace which passes all understanding. We pray especially today for Israel and Lebanon, for Iraq and Afghanistan and for our own country.

- Filled with compassion, gracious Father, you have given us the gift of relationships so that we need never face loneliness and so that we may blossom through each other. Help us so to absorb the Bread of Life that we feel genuine concern for those who have no good relationships, and give us the motivation to offer those people our honest friendship. May we use the opportunities you have given us through our families and friends, to learn to genuinely love each other, in good times and in bad.

- Heavenly Father, as we look to the future, we bring into your presence those of our friends and families who are sick, who need to know you and feel you within the very depths of their being. Lay your healing hands upon them as we name them in our own hearts.

- Loving God, be with the sad, the lonely and the bereaved as you pour out your love and comfort on them. Father, enable the sad to find some happiness, the lonely companionship and the bereaved comfort knowing that, through believing in your Son, their loved ones are safe in your eternal Kingdom. Bless each one of us this day and always.

- We ask these prayers through him who died so that all this might be possible for us, Jesus Christ our Lord. Amen.

Offertory Prayer

REV. WENDY DRAKE

This offering now we bring to you, O God,
as a tangible expression of our love;
received from you and shared with each other,
regardless of anything except our common humanity
and your eternal divinity.
Make real in our hearts and lives, our hands and actions
something of our living Lord.
In his name, we ask all our prayers.   AMEN.

General Intercessions

REV. PAULINE STEENBERGEN

This Intercession could be used any time, any place, anywhere. This one is 'ready to wear'. Sometimes it's a relief to find something in a book that can be instantly used. It works particularly well in All-Age services.

When questions, worry, stress, busyness crush our
    spirits
Let your Way of calm and gentleness soothe us
Jesus, teach us how to cope when we feel stuck

When hospitals admit, test, operate, treat or nurse
Let your Way of healing flow through healing hands
Jesus, touch those struggling with ill health today

When accidents happen on roads, rails, waters, skies
Let your Way of rescue quickly reach the scene
Jesus, alert us to danger as we travel

When there is fear after theft, violence, bullying,
Let your Way of justice overcome
**Jesus, make us stand up for what is right, true and
    good**

When there are tears after death, separation or rejection
Let your Way of hope bring strength
Jesus, comfort the broken-hearted at this time

When borders are violent and guns loaded
Let your Way of peace cease human hostility
**Jesus, hear our prayers for the Middle East, Iraq, India
and Pakistan**

When we question ourselves and face our flaws
When loving or even liking others feels impossible
Jesus, give us your Spirit to become more like you

Jesus: you went to God with your questions.
You asked 'why?'
**In the silence, we bring you all we want to ask today
And we listen to all you ask of us** ... *(silence)*

Hear our prayers ...
We await your answers. AMEN.

Introit and Dismissal for Family Service

REV. MARY HENDERSON

Before Call to Worship

Toddlers, toddle! Lovers, leap!
Tired teenagers, stir from sleep!
Grannies, gather! Zimmers, zing!
Dancers, dazzle! Singers, sing!
All and sundry, gather near.
Come and worship – God is here!

After Benediction

Now skedaddle. Leave your pew!
God has work for you to do!
Service done (but just beginning),
Lots of love – and no more sinning!
Up the town or in the square,
Go and join him – God is there!

Part Two

THE INSPIRATION BEHIND THE *WORSHIP ANTHOLOGY*

Breaking the Mould

REV. KATHY GALLOWAY

In November 2006, Rowan Williams, the Archbishop of Canterbury, gave an interview that was widely quoted, and equally widely misrepresented, as suggesting that the ordination of women in the Church of England might one day be revisited, even repealed. Many of its women priests felt damned with faint praise when he said:

> I don't think it [the ordination of women] has transformed or renewed the Church of England in spectacular ways. Equally, I don't think it has corrupted or ruined the Church of England in spectacular ways. It has somehow got into the bloodstream and I don't give it a second thought these days, in terms of regular worship.

Though I am quite sure that no slight was intended, it would be difficult to argue that this constitutes a resounding affirmation of the ordination of women! Many ordained women in Scotland were sympathetic. But the affair also raised the question: 'Does this somehow apply to us too?'

The processes leading up to women's ordination in the Church of Scotland and the Church of England were somewhat different. There were a number of unsuccessful attempts to raise the issue throughout the first half of the twentieth century. Then, in 1963, Mary Lusk (later Levison) petitioned the Assembly to test her call to ministry. Thereafter, it took five years for the Church of Scotland to agree to ordain women on the same basis as men. When Mary stood at the bar of the Assembly, she was cutting a rather solitary path. Though women were, as always, exercising ministry within the Church, only a handful had the necessary theological training for ordination. When I studied divinity in Glasgow in the early 1970s, there were fewer than ten women out of more than 100; and, when I was ordained in 1977, I was still in the first dozen. So, the numbers actually ordained in the first ten years were tiny.

In the Church of England, however, it took fourteen years from the first motion to ordain women, proposed in 1978, until the success of a similar motion in 1992. This gave many more women the opportunity to pursue training. In the first year alone, hundreds were ordained. Furthermore, though there was considerable support for women's ordination in Scotland, it was never formally organised on anything like the scale of the Movement for the Ordination of Women in England.

The Scotswomen were ordained into a masculine model of ministry, and so few were they in the early years that the likelihood of changing this model dramatically was remote. Indeed, some did not wish to change the model; their struggle was not primarily based on factors of gender, rather on the confirmation of individual vocation. They did not seek to emphasise female distinctiveness, and often sought to minimise any suggestion of gender difference in ministry. For them, the important recognition was one of personhood, of equal ability to do the same job in the same way, in which distinctiveness would be attributable to many factors including individual personality. They would perhaps agree with Rowan Williams, and not feel at all slighted by his words, which were essentially: 'business as usual'.

Others might have liked the model to be a bit more flexible, especially when it came to the surprising fact that women get pregnant. But, lacking numbers and any kind of organised movement, and perhaps with the caution of 'new girls' and the awareness that anything they did would be scrutinised and judged as representative, they just put their heads down, worked hard and did the job to the best of their considerable ability. Improvements in working conditions and rights for ordained women, such as job-sharing and maternity rights, have tended to come through individual women pursuing cases and setting precedents, reflecting the juridical governance of the Church of Scotland.

In England, the impact of a flood rather than a trickle was more immediate and more threatening. Moreover, the changed social climate in Britain between 1968 and 1992 meant that women were being ordained in a very different context. Jean Mayland wrote:

> When Mary Levison wrestled to become a minister only one skeleton fell out of the cupboard – that of ordination. In the Church of England, all the skeletons have fallen out at once: priesthood, ordination, inclusive language, the motherhood of God, issues of sexuality. It has made the battle long and bitter, but it has enabled us to put all our cards on the table and to have a chance to break masculine moulds of ministry. (See Bibliography: in Macdonald (ed.), pp. 47–8)

Of course, this reflects some of the ecclesiological and cultural differences between the two churches. But two different and major strands of feminism are clearly recognisable here. The first minimised gender differences, emphasised equality and mounted political challenges. The second valued gender differences, emphasised inclusion of difference and mounted theological challenges. That the strands are so evident is a reminder that the ordination of women in both churches was part of one of the most important global social movements of the twentieth century. God may have been calling individual women to ordination; but, without the effect of the women's movement, there would have been no-one to agree. After all, there had been no-one to agree for the best part of 2,000 years!

In her book, *Wrestling with the Church*, Mary Levison said that she had never had to campaign or to fight with her church. Many ordained women in the Church of Scotland would agree with her. The theological challenges of the full inclusion of women in the Church were mostly taken up in Scotland by lay women. As a very young minister, struggling to discover what it meant to minister as a woman, and finding no real movement or solidarity among ordained women, I received enormous support, encouragement and inspiration from lay women, first in the Woman's Guild but also, as time went on, from ecumenical and civic women's networks such as NEWS, the YWCA and the Scottish Convention of Women. The 'skeletons' that fell into the arms of the movement for the ordination of women in England were primarily confronted in Scotland by lay women – and they certainly had to campaign! In the midst of our own pioneering and sometimes very painful struggles, I am not sure that we women ministers have always properly appreciated and acknowledged the debt we owe to lay women, women elders and women deacons in the cultural and theological changes that have supported our ministries.

Today, forty years on, Scottish women live in a society where equal opportunities are an accepted part of working life, where good practice requires looking critically at unexamined assumptions, and where changing patterns of family life have led to much greater role diversity among men and women. That is not to say that either full equality or full inclusion has been achieved. It is one thing to change legislation, another to change institutional cultures, as women have discovered in every walk of life, not just the Church. When it is not being intentional about changing the settings, the Church's default position is still male-dominated and designed. But we do not have to put up with 'flying' bishops undermining our very existence. Our equality model has meant that we are not corralled into non-stipendiary jobs; and there are now no roles or offices in the Church of Scotland closed to women.

The ordination of women has never been about breaking through the 'stained-glass ceiling'. It has mattered because who the minister is speaks to the **Church**. There are messages of value encoded in where we attribute spiritual leadership. The ordination of women has been a significant affirmation of the value and experience of women in the life of the Church.

It has mattered because who the minister is speaks to **women**. No woman can speak for all women. Their ministries are as diverse and distinctive as their male colleagues, and gifts fairly evenly distributed regardless of gender. But their ordination has helped to redress the long failure to offer to women, including those who have served the Church devotedly in entirely traditional ways, the respect, dignity and equality of persons equally created in the image of God.

And it speaks to those **outside** about the Church today. Times have changed since the Church of Scotland was a major power in the land and assumed that it could speak to and for Scotland. But perhaps that is no bad thing, this shifting of authority to areas where women offer so much – in sensitive pastoral care, worship leadership, intellectual rigour, organisational competence, community development, imaginative spirituality and the ability to lead, nurture and encourage congregations, often in the most difficult places. Outwards to the lunch clubs, playgroups and neighbourhood schemes, to the support projects for homeless people, asylum-seekers, survivors of domestic violence and sexual abuse, to the racial justice and anti-poverty initiatives, to the Church without walls. These things more truthfully reflect the reality of Church of Scotland life today and model its greatest strengths.

So, I celebrate forty years of not accepting the minimisation of the gifts of women in ministry, but rather the lifting up of all the gifts of the people of God. Women have not accepted that what we bring to the churches is unworthy of the churches' time and energy; we have acted like we belong because we do belong. And I celebrate forty years of ministry filled with the Gospel spirit of hope and compassion.

The Last Word

REV. MARGARET FORRESTER

The 1960s were 'swinging'; certainly they were different. To understand, we must look at the context. We had survived a horrendous war. We had endured food, fuel and clothes rationing. We were challenged by the resultant sense of equality. We had watched the dissolution of the British Empire. We rejoiced in the welfare state. We saw the proliferation of new universities. Young people and women wanted to be heard.

It is difficult for young folk now to understand how acquiescent women were in the 1950s. It was before feminism and liberation theology. It was before Germaine Greer's *The Female Eunuch* or Betty Friedan's *The Feminine Mystique*. In the 1950s, there were reserved places at universities for ex-servicemen. The effect was that, in all subjects, but especially science, engineering and medical subjects, the quotas for women were tiny. I understand that the Highers (the Scottish School Leaving Certificate) had a lower pass mark for boys in all subjects, making entrance to universities harder for girls.

All courts of the Church of Scotland were composed of men. The contribution of the Church of Scotland's Woman's Guild in education and fundraising was outstanding. But suggestions that women may share in the decisions of the Church were greeted with suspicion. There had been movement in other denominations: the Presbyterian Church of England, the Congregational Unions in Scotland and in England and Wales, and the United Free Church all ordained women. The World Council of Churches commissioned

Dr Kathleen Bliss, an Anglican, to evaluate the life and work of women in the Church. Her book *The Service and Status of Women in the Churches* (SCM Press, 1952) was an ecumenical milestone. The University of Aberdeen conferred a DD on her, the first woman to be so honoured.

In the Church of Scotland, the Marchioness of Aberdeen had raised the issue in 1931. For thirty-eight years, on and off, the quaintly named Committee on the Place of Women in the Church worried at the issue that was not going to go away. Meantime, women like Dr Elizabeth Hewat served abroad, first in China then as Professor in Wilson College, Bombay. She took a BD and then wrote her doctoral thesis on a comparison of the sayings of Confucius and the poetry of the Psalms. 'There was no-one', she recalled with a twinkle in her eye, 'who was competent in both ancient Chinese and Hebrew, so I had to have extra examiners.' By and large, the Church of Scotland did not recognise her gifts; Edinburgh University did, by conferring on her a DD.

As late as 1961, I asked the Principal of New College, Edinburgh, Professor J. H. S. Burleigh, about his views on the ordination of women. His reply was: 'It's coming. But not in my lifetime, I hope. It won't be this century, anyway.' Increasingly, there were concerns that the gifts of women were being ignored. This was challenge and opportunity. As so often, there were those who feared change and opposed any innovation. For those of us who felt the call to ministry, we knew rejection and hurt. But we also met grace and generosity. My underlying memory is of joy that we were caught up in God's plan for renewal.

Towards the end of the 1950s, there emerged a group of women who, having been born, baptised, nurtured and confirmed within the Church of Scotland, believed that their ministerial vocation also lay within the Church of Scotland. Foremost among them was Mary Lusk (later Levison). It is difficult to overestimate the debt that all women ministers owe to her.

She has told her own story in *Wrestling with the Church* (Arthur James Ltd, 1992). After graduating from Oxford and Edinburgh,

Mary offered her services to the Church of Scotland. She was commissioned as a deaconess in 1954. Three years later, she was licensed to preach. For a few years, the Church of Scotland had a handful of theologically trained women who were commissioned as deaconesses with licence to preach – a strange theological anomaly. I think the second woman to be licensed was Margaret Allan, who went into religious education. I was probably the third, closely followed by Sheila White (now Spence).

In 1963, Mary Lusk, Assistant Chaplain at Edinburgh University, petitioned the General Assembly of the Church of Scotland to test her call. The Moderator, the Very Rev. James S. Stewart, was in the chair throughout the debate on that Saturday afternoon. Did he ever get to the traditional Garden Party, I wonder? The official minute is sparse, belying the intensity of feelings on both sides. While some of the arguments against granting the crave of the petition had an attempt at theology, some bordered on the insulting. Clearly, there were those who feared that the Church would change for ever. It was impossible for us students, tightly packed in the gallery with deaconesses and friends, to refrain from cheering and stamping the speeches. With magisterial quiet, the Moderator declared that the galleries would be cleared if there was not silence. At one point, an elderly gentleman, moving so slowly that he had to be helped up to the podium, opened his mouth to speak. Our hearts sank within us. At his age, he had to be conservative. 'We have just admitted these men from other churches ...' he waved his hands dismissively – and then with a great roar he continued: 'and none of them can hold a candle to her. Ordain her, I say, and ordain her now!' The roar of agreement reverberated around the rafters, and the gallery shook with fervent feet. That time, the galleries were spoken to so severely that we spent the rest of the debate in utter silence. After proposals and debate, finally, a sympathetic counter-motion was passed 'instructing the [Church's] Panel on Doctrine to give consideration to the Petition and its crave when it is dealing with the Place of Women in the Church and to report to the next General Assembly'. We knew that history was being made.

I was at New College from 1961 to 1964. It was built for men; there were no designated lavatories for women. It was built for men in other ways. A degree was one thing; to become a candidate for the ministry was impossible. It became a game. We had to find out what extra things the candidates were up to. So we sat the mandatory Greek New Testament and annual Bible exams. Each year, we were assured with a sigh that these were not strictly necessary. But we did them. We took extra classes in Church Law and Homiletics. All the men were assigned as student assistants in the second year. I remember hammering on the door of Professor Tindal's office, begging him to find an assistantship for me. Many ministers refused point blank to take a woman. I had an extraordinarily happy year at Salisbury Parish Church with Rev. Robert Taylor. Sheila White, if I recall correctly, was with Rev. Fred Levison of St Bernard's-Davidson.

Some staff were consistently helpful and encouraging, such as Professors Stewart and Porteous, and Robin Barbour. Others were less than supportive. A few students were unbelievably insulting. 'Women don't have the brains for Hebrew.' 'Why should we have women ministers or elders when we have enough men?' 'Women don't have strong enough voices.' I felt smug when I won the prize (a cheque for £3.00) for excellence in the public reading of the Bible.

The real arguments had to be theological – biblical, historical, ecumenical. I read everything I could lay my hands on and spent a lot of time speaking to Woman's Guild meetings or Youth Fellowships. Occasionally, a few elders would come in and sit at the back; many is the useful chat I had with doubting elders over tea and biscuits.

Immediately before the 1967 General Assembly, wearied by excuses, a group of us – Mary Levison (née Lusk), Elizabeth Hewat, Margaret Forrester, Sheila White, Mary Weir and Claude Barbour – prepared an open letter to the General Assembly. This was released at a press conference during the Assembly. The press coverage was considerable. Days later, following a proposal by

Rev. Grahame Bailey, seconded by Professor Robin Barbour, a Draft Overture was agreed and sent down under the Barrier Act. The following year, just after I had given birth to our second child in India, the Act was passed.

It would be good to report that all was then plain sailing; but life is not like that. The first woman to be ordained was Rev. Elizabeth McConnachie, a retired deaconess who had taken a BD. She worked without taking a salary. Sometimes there is something deeply ungenerous in the Church! For years, perhaps still, vacancy committees were heard to mutter 'no women ministers'. It is a matter of fact that women were called to challenging parishes – isolated, inner-city housing schemes. City-centre congregations and suburban charges are still slow to contemplate a woman minister.

In 1980, when I was called to St Michael's Church in Edinburgh, it was a part-time terminable appointment. 'You were the best of a bad lot', the convenor of the vacancy committee grumbled. 'When we got you, we were scraping the bottom of the barrel.' The elder and I became friends, and seventeen years later I took his funeral.

The Church, both in individual members and in its courts, can be ungenerous, slow to see God's gracious call, unwilling to change, quick to condemn. Thank God, there are some people willing to knock on doors and rattle cages. God is always calling the Church to renewal, to show love, to welcome, to forgive, to manifest grace and joy and delight in our life and work. In celebrating that day in 1968, let us give thanks and listen to God calling us now, to new tasks, new vision, new decisions. And to God be the glory.

The Story of This Book

The Inspiration behind *Worship Anthology*: 'Life Begins at 40'

> Moderator, Fathers, Brethren ... I believe myself called of God to the Ministry of Word and Sacraments ... and that this call be examined and dealt with in whatever way the Church may see fit.
>
> (Mary Levison, *Wrestling with the Church*, p. 66)

This is the voice of Mary Lusk. A very lone female voice petitioning an all-male General Assembly in the Church of Scotland in Edinburgh on Saturday 25 May 1963.

Can we imagine ourselves in that moment? She was a 40-year-old graduate of Oxford University and New College, Edinburgh. A trained deaconess licensed to preach and a serving Chaplain at the University of Edinburgh. She was given fifteen minutes to lodge her petition. Mary was making a personal plea based on her own strength of calling. Yet, to make this moment all the more terrifying was the knowledge that she was also knocking at the doors of the Church in the hope that they would open up to allow many, many more women to pursue their own call to the Ministry of Word and Sacraments. What an awesome responsibility! 1963 would not be the year that a decision would be made. In 1966, the Assembly decided that women could be ordained to eldership. Yet it would be five years after Mary's original petition until the Assembly granted permission for women to be ordained to Word and Sacraments. The date of this landmark decision was Wednesday 22 May 1968.

The publication of this book in May 2008 marks the ruby anniversary of that historic moment. Over the forty-year period, women have been able to fulfil their calling, training and ordination in Church of Scotland parishes and appointments all over Scotland, Europe and overseas. There are currently almost 200 employed in the Kirk in this way. Rev. Margaret Forrester remembers when she could fit all her female colleagues in her front living room! Her 'Last Word' is a fascinating perspective from a woman who has been working in the Church prior to and long after the 1968 watershed.

The editorial team for this book are four Church of Scotland ministers. We worked together as an all-female team in Ellon Parish Church between 1999 and 2006. Foreseeing the fortieth anniversary approaching, we thought that this marker would be the ideal opportunity to pay tribute and express gratitude to those who made our ordination possible in the past and to celebrate the ministry of ordained women in the Church of Scotland today. What better way to do so than to invite all our female colleagues to contribute their own original material to a worship anthology, which would be launched to commemorate May 1968! So, in February 2007, we asked for unique, tried and tested material. We received a vast array of contributions from diverse ministry contexts. A glance at the contents page reveals that each contributor selected has something unique, precious and special to offer.

As worship leaders, we greatly enjoyed training and enabling all ages to use their gifts in worship in Ellon Parish Church. We wanted this book to be by women but enjoyable and useable by everyone in personal devotions, or small-group study as well as public worship for the glory of God. Our highest hope is that this publication will bring all ages of lay and ordained, male and female together as each contribution is made use of throughout the ruby-anniversary year of 2008 and beyond.

Finally, we are thrilled that the launch of this book coincides happily with the end of the Very Rev. Sheilagh Kesting's moderatorial year. Sheilagh is the first woman ordained to Word and Sacrament who has become Moderator of the General Assembly of the Church of Scotland and therefore the first to celebrate Communion for the Assembly, on 21 May 2007. We are delighted to include prayers by Sheilagh from that week. However, Sheilagh is not the first woman Moderator. In May 2004, Dr Alison Elliot became the first elder and thereby the first woman to become Moderator of the General Assembly of the Church of Scotland. It is with her and all other lay women and men that we celebrate the huge contribution made to the life and work of the Church by people with different gifts. All have played, and continue to play, a vital role in our journey. Kathy Galloway, in her piece, expresses this passionately and profoundly.

Another happy coincidence is that our launch coincides with the month of Christian Aid week, and we are pleased that Christian Aid has agreed to accept our royalties.

We are very, very chuffed with our book! What was just an idea on the night of a friend's ordination and induction has grown into something we can hold, read and use. It's a book by which we ourselves are inspired, excited, moved, taught, encouraged and helped. Most of all, it's a book for which we are grateful. We appreciate that this anthology represents the ongoing work by our sisters in Christ, whose calling, experiences, ministries and creativity are precious and valuable and are making a significant impact in building up Christ's Kingdom. To them, and to all women ordained to Word and Sacraments, we want to say to you:

> HAPPY ANNIVERSARY! Glory be to God for your calling, ordination and service. May 2008 be the year that the whole church remembers, affirms and encourages all women ordained to Word and Sacrament, and may we never take for granted how the permission to be ordained was achieved.

Sheila   Pauline   Alison   Eleanor

Co-Editors:
Rev. Sheila Craggs
(Presbytery of Gordon, Church of Scotland)
Rev. Eleanor Macalister
(Presbytery of Gordon, Church of Scotland)
Rev. Alison Mehigan
(Presbytery of Moray, Church of Scotland)
Rev. Pauline Steenbergen
(Presbytery of Annandale and Eskdale, Church of Scotland)

Christian Aid website: www.surefish.co.uk

Acknowledgements

- To our family and friends who patiently shared our first editorial journey.

- To our priceless men: Tom Craggs, Gary Macalister, John Mehigan and David Pitkeathly. You know all the reasons why we needed you!

- To Rev. Steve Emery. Your ordination and induction was the end of our matriarchal ministry and the trigger for our vision of the Ruby Book.

- To all at Ellon Parish Church. Your friendship, financial assistance, use of office and equipment and 'believing without seeing' (not to mention your ministry to the four wifie ministers) has been awesome.

- To Ellon Academy for photocopying.

- To Angela Buchan and Ben P. for help with the mailing.

- To Susan Reid at People Solutions for team-building and always 'being there' by e-mail and text.

- To Alison Murray at 121 for always knowing the answer.

- To Marjory Clark and Kate Tuckett at Christian Aid. We are thrilled to be in partnership with you and to know that this book will make a difference to your work.

- To Ann Crawford. Thank you for saying 'yes' and for sharing the vision and letting us run with it.

- To Richard Allen, particularly for sterling support at the General Assembly 2007 fringe event, and to Saint Andrew Press, who did us proud with the organising of refreshments for all who came through the Senate Room door.
- To all our contributors. There would be no book without you.
- To Sheilagh, Margaret and Kathy: your care, advice and encouragement is deeply appreciated.
- Thank you Karen, Carol and Caroline for being a huge help in the Senate Room. (Chocolate heaven!)
- Finally, to Mary Levison. Words cannot do justice to the gratitude we feel for your faith, calling, courage and confidence to petition the Assembly on 25 May 1963. We dedicate this book to you, Mary. Thank you ... 'Happy Ruby Anniversary!'

Contributors' Biographies

Dorothy Anderson

Dorothy was born and educated in Edinburgh and spent many years as a solicitor in Edinburgh's New Town. After many years as a Sunday School teacher, she began training for the ministry in 2001 and was ordained as Outreach Minister in early 2006 in the Parish Church of St Andrew and St George in Edinburgh.

Susan Anderson

Susan was brought up in the Church of England, married a Scot and moved to Scotland in 1975. Her first career was as a piano teacher, and then she retrained as a clinical liaison officer for the Epilepsy Association. Around 1990, Susan felt the call to ministry. Susan is minister of St John's in Kilmarnock.

Anne Attenburrow

Anne is an Auxiliary Minister and was ordained in October 2006 following a career in medicine. Anne is presently Auxiliary Minister acting as Parish Assistant at Elgin High linked with Pluscarden and Birnie.

Sandra Black

Sandra was ordained in 1988, moved to Glasgow in 1997 and was inducted to Toryglen at the beginning of 2003. Sandra is married to David, who is also a Parish Minister, and they have a daughter, Lucy.

Lynn Brady

Lynn was ordained in 1996 to parishes in the West Mainland of Orkney, but has spent her last five years of ministry as Parish Minister of Abdie and Dunbog linked with Newburgh in Fife.

Jill Clancy

Jill, at the age of 30, was ordained and inducted as Parish Minister into St John's Church, Gourock, in the year 2000.

Sheila Craggs

Sheila is an Auxiliary Minister ordained in September 1997. After three years in America, where Sheila had the opportunity to work in a church, she returned to Scotland, continued her ministry in Ellon Parish Church, and retired in 2007.

Joan Craig

Joan was called to the Presbytery of Orkney in 1993 (until 2005) to the linked charge of Deerness, Holm and St Andrews – united in 2004 as East Mainland Church.

Christine Creegan

Christine is a part-time Associate Minister in Pitlochry. She came into ministry late in life, and spent seven years in Newtonhill and then five years at Grantully, Logierait and Strathtay.

Liz Crumlish

Liz has been married for twenty-five years and has two children. Her ambition is to major in delinquency and learn to laugh at herself! Previously a Hospital Chaplain, Liz, like so many ministers, has been there for families in all their highs and lows. Liz is now Parish Minister in Inverkip.

Jane Denniston

Married to a minister, Jane was ordained in 2001. Previously, she was a Regional Development Worker, then National Advisor in

Adult Education with the Board of Parish Education. Currently, she works with candidates in training for ministry.

Rachel Dobie

Rachel was ordained in 1991 and was previously a Reader and Sunday School advisor. She is happily married and has two grown-up children. Rachel is minister of Broughton, Glenholm and Kilbucho linked with Skirling linked with Stobo and Drumelzier linked with Tweedsmuir in the beautiful Border area of Melrose and Peebles.

Elspeth Dougall

Elspeth was ordained in 1989 by the Presbyterian Church of East Africa. She spent two years as Chaplain at Alliance Girls' High School near Nairobi. In 1991, Elspeth was inducted to joint ministry at Marchmont St Giles'. Since her retirement, she and her husband have continued to live in Edinburgh.

Wendy Drake

Married with two adult children, and one of a family of ministers, Wendy says she 'was called to a life on the parish front and so far am still fighting on it'. She was minister of Cockpen and Carrington linked with Lasswade linked with Rosewell until she retired in 2007.

Carol Ford

Called to ministry in middle age (her words!), Carol was previously a drama teacher. She was also actively involved in her home church as an elder and convenor of its worship committee. Carol is minister of St Margaret's Parish Church in Edinburgh.

Margaret Forrester

Margaret studied at Edinburgh University, gaining her MA in 1961 and her BD in 1964. She was then commissioned as Deaconess and licensed to preach in 1964. She has served the Church for more than four decades. Her call to serve has taken her from Scotland to India, India to Sussex and then back to Scotland. She retired from St Michael's, Edinburgh, in 2003, and has served with the Overseas Council and the Board of World Mission and Unity. She writes regularly for *Expository Times*, and her most recent work in 2007 is *The Cat Who Decided*, a book for children. Margaret is married with two children and five grandchildren.

Elsie Fortune

Elsie has family members in both east and west Scotland but is very happy in Aberdeen as the manse family. She is married to Eric, and they have one daughter. Elsie has a background in chemistry and worked for some years for the Rowett Research Institute. She was ordained and inducted as Parish Minister of St Mary's Parish Church in Aberdeen in November 2003.

Shirley Fraser

Shirley is presently part-time Field Director with Friends International and also in part-time Locumships. Previously, Shirley was minister at St George's Tillydrone Church in Aberdeen from 1992 until 2001.

Rosie Frew

Ordained in 1988, Rosie was minister of Largo and Newburn linked with Largo St David's until 1995, when she became minister of Abbotshall Parish Church, Kirkcaldy. Rosie is married and has two children.

Kathy Galloway

Kathy is the Leader of the Iona Community. She is a practical theologian, campaigner and writer and was ordained as a Church of Scotland minister in 1977. After three years in parish ministry in Edinburgh, she set up the Edinburgh Peace and Justice Centre for Scottish Churches Council and since then has always worked ecumenically. Most recently, she was employed by Church Action on Poverty. She is the author of nine books of theology, liturgy and poetry, and her writings have been widely anthologised. She is a patron of the Student Christian Movement.

Liz Gibson

Liz is married with two teenage sons. Before coming into ministry, Liz lived in Edinburgh, working backstage in theatre and then in bookselling. She is a member of the Iona Community. Liz is Associate Minister in Kilmore and Oban and is also Hospital Chaplain at Lorn and Islands District General Hospital.

Mary Haddow

Mary is minister of Banchory East in Aberdeenshire. Her husband is a great supporter and encourager. They have two children.

Karen Harbison

At the 'Fringe Event' at the General Assembly in May 2007, we were welcomed by the aroma of a chocolate fountain! Karen's all-age worship service is guaranteed to enable children, young people and adults to explore the overflowing, generous love of God. Karen is minister of Hamilton Trinity.

Mary Henderson

Mary was ordained in 1990 and has been Associate Minister in Dollar linked with Muckhart linked with Glendevon since 2005.

Yvonne Hendrie

Yvonne is married to Rev. Brian Hendrie and is the mother of Chloe. The family lives at Whitehills near Banff. She was previously minister of Hawick Congregational Church and has also worked in several hospitals and hospices. Yvonne is without a charge at present but writes extensively for *Roots Worship*. Yvonne has recently been appointed Chaplain to Turriff Cottage Hospital.

Evelyn Hope

Evelyn was born in 1934. On leaving Shawlands Academy at the age of 18, she wanted to be a minister. In those days, of course, there was no possibility for her to fulfil this desire, and so she trained to become a radiographer, working in Malawi in the late 1960s. She then trained as a social worker. At the age of 50, she was made redundant. With the call to ministry still there, she entered Glasgow University, studied for a BD and was ordained at Thornlie Parish Church in Wishaw in 1990. Evelyn retired in 1998 and worships in South Shawlands Parish Church.

Alison Hutchison

Born and brought up in and around Edinburgh and Midlothian, Alison went on to study at New College and has been a Hospital and Hospice Chaplain in Aberdeen, full and part-time, for almost twenty years. Alison is married with children and lives in Aberdeenshire.

Alison Jack

Alison is the Hope Trust Research Fellow at New College, Edinburgh University.

Tina Kemp

Tina was ordained as an Auxiliary Minister in May 2005 and is attached to the West Kirk of Helensburgh, part of a parish grouping of three churches. She has been a journalist for twenty-eight years and works for a local newspaper in Dumbarton.

Lezley Kennedy

Lezley was ordained in 2000 following studies at St Andrew's, Princeton and Edinburgh. As well as being minister of Dundee: Downfield South Parish Church, she serves on the Ministries Council.

Sheilagh Kesting

Born and brought up in Stornoway, Isle of Lewis, Sheilagh gained a general Arts degree at Edinburgh University and an honours degree in Philosophy of Religion at New College, Edinburgh. She served as Parish Minister in Overtown Parish Church, Wishaw and St Andrew's High Church, Musselburgh. Since 1993, she has been the secretary to the General Assembly's Committee on Ecumenical Relations. She was appointed Moderator of the General Assembly, May 2007 to 2008.

Rosemary Legge

Rosemary was brought up in India. Her first degree was a BSc in engineering at Imperial College, and she subsequently worked as an engineer. Following studies at Northumbria Bible College, a BD in London and MTh at Aberdeen University, Rosemary was ordained to the Church of Scotland ministry in 1992. She is married and is presently minister of Grantully, Logierait and Strathtay.

Maureen Leitch

Maureen is married and has two grown-up children. Maureen studied at New College, Edinburgh University and has been minister in Barrhead: Bourock Parish Church for twelve years.

Anne Lithgow

After two years as Associate Minister in Gilmerton, Edinburgh, Anne was inducted in 1994 to the rural parish of Dunglass spanning the boundary between East Lothian and Berwickshire. Anne is married with three grown-up children.

Anne Logan

Anne, a daughter of the manse, was ordained in 1981 and is married with two grown-up sons. She and her husband enjoy sailing out of the west coast of Scotland, a passion for which Anne would like to have more time. Anne is minister of Stockbridge in Edinburgh.

Eleanor Macalister

Ordained in 1994, Eleanor was Associate Minister of Ellon Parish Church for five years and was then called to that charge as Parish Minister, serving in that capacity for almost eight years. On 31 October 2006, she took an elective early retirement from parish ministry. Eleanor is married with two grown-up children and is still actively involved in the Church.

Moyna McGlynn

Moyna has published academic work on the apocryphal book *The Wisdom of Solomon*. She is also a part-time lecturer, teaching on the biblical world, for the Scottish Baptist College at the University of the West of Scotland. Moyna has been the minister of Eastwood Parish Church since 1999 and is married with three grown-up children.

Gillean Maclean

Gillean would like us all to know that she is married to a very nice man, has three daughters and has very probably the two most beautiful grandchildren in the world! Gillean is parish minister of St John's Oxgangs, Edinburgh.

Marjory MacLean

Marjory was Parish Minister in Stromness, Orkney before becoming full-time Depute Clerk of the General Assembly. Her pastoral ministry is found now in Royal Naval Reserve Chaplaincy.

Edith McMillan

Edith has been an ordained minister since 1981, working in Shetland and in various ministries in Dundee. She is currently Associate Minister in a team ministry in Douglas and Mid Craigie linked with Craigiebank Church.

Alison Mehigan

Alison felt called to ministry as a teenager but first of all followed a fourteen-year career in the oil and gas industry and four years in academia before finally responding to her call. She was ordained and inducted in October 2003 to Bellie linked with Speymouth in Moray. She is married to John, and they have two children.

Jean Montgomerie

Jean was ordained and inducted to Peterculter: Kelman Memorial Parish Church in January 1973, and served there until August 1998, when she moved to Forfar: St Margaret's Parish Church. During the period of her ministry, she was Convenor of the Board of Ministry for six years and of the Board of Communication for four and a half years. Jean retired in January 2006 and lives in Peterculter.

Catriona Ogilvie

Catriona says this about her life and her ministry: 'I have been ordained for eight years. Before this crazy, exhausting, wonderful job I was a childminder, and before that, a social worker. But most importantly, I was, and still am, "Ministry Mum" to three sons, now in their twenties, who keep my feet on the ground.' Catriona is minister of Cumbernauld: Old Parish Church.

Carleen Robertson

Carleen is minister of Eassie and Nevay linked with Newtyle in the Presbytery of Angus. She enjoys reading other people's meditations and likes 'mucking about' with words when she has the time. She is a devoted fan of Leonard Cohen, whose words inspire her.

Sarah Ross

When Sarah submitted her article, she had just finished seven months' maternity leave and was also just two years into her first charge. Despite those challenges, she still found time to contribute to the book. Sarah is minister of Forth: St Paul's, an ex-mining community in Lanarkshire.

Lindsay Schluter

Ordained in 1995, Lindsay is minister of Trinity Parish Church, Larkhall.

Christine Sime

Born and bred in Edinburgh, Christine had a first career in molecular biology, working in research. Her faith and church life started in her late twenties. She was ordained and inducted in 1994 to her present charge of Dunscore with Glencairn and Moniaive.

Pauline Steenbergen

Pauline experienced a calling to ordained ministry at the age of 16 and has been training and working in churches ever since. She was Parish Minister in St Luke's and Queen Street, Broughty Ferry and Associate Minister in Ellon Parish Church. She is married to Rev. David Pitkeathly, and they have one son called Ben. Currently, she is a Congregational Facilitator living in Carlisle.

Margaret Stein

Born and brought up in Aberdeenshire, Margaret studied at Edinburgh Art College and then New College, Edinburgh. She is married to Rev. Jock Stein, and was ordained in 1984 as an Auxiliary Minister in Dundee. She has been part-time warden at Carberry Tower, Musselburgh, and is presently part-time minister at Tulliallan and Kincardine, work-sharing with her husband.

Caroline Taylor

Caroline is minister of St Athernase Church, Leuchars. Her early working life was spent as a secretary, which was very satisfying and enjoyable.

Gayle Taylor

Ordained in 1999, Gayle has been minister of Bishopton Parish Church since then. She has a strong background in summer mission and youth work, and is always very passionate about involving young people in thinking about, preparing and leading worship.

Shirley Thomas

Shirley was confirmed in the Church of England in 1955. She worked as a medical social worker at St George's Hospital and then went to Bible college in 1964 for two years. She was a missionary in Nepal from 1966 to 1984. She was ordained as an Auxiliary Minister in 2000 and retired in 2006.

Jenny Williams

Jenny Williams is currently Chaplain to the Christian Fellowship of Healing – an ecumenical voluntary organisation committed to offering listening and healing prayer to people of all faiths and none, and to resourcing churches and individual Christians in healing and prayer ministry work. Jenny is a full member of Edinburgh Presbytery and has regularly contributed to *Pray Now* over the past seven years.

Mary Wilson

Mary was a Church of Scotland missionary nurse with the United Church of Northern India from 1958 to 1969. In 1990, she was ordained to the Ministry of Word and Sacrament. She has served as an Auxiliary Minister in Lothian, and then Sutherland, and then Dunkeld and Meigle.

Julie Woods

In September 2005, Julie was ordained and inducted as minister of Elgin: High linked with Birnie and Pluscarden, where there is an opportunity for her dream of team ministry to be fulfilled. She is married to Robert, and they have three sons.

Evie Young

Prior to retiring, Evie was Parish Minister firstly in Larbert West and then Kilmun (St Munn's) linked with Strone and Ardentinny. She was Secretary to the Committee on Education for the Ministry for six years, working in the Church of Scotland offices at 121 George Street, Edinburgh. Her work helped young parents coming from different church backgrounds to feel included in the Church of Scotland family to which they had now chosen to belong.

Bibliography

We share with you the books by, for, contributed to or edited by women which have inspired and guided us on our editorial journey.

Blackie, Nansie (ed.), *A Time for Trumpets* (Edinburgh: Saint Andrew Press, 2005).

Boom, Corrie ten, *Tramp for the Lord* (London: Hodder & Stoughton, 1976).

Forrester, Duncan B., David S. M. Hamilton, Alan Main and James A. Whyte (eds), *Worship Now II* (Edinburgh: Saint Andrew Press, 1989).

Forrester, Margaret, *Touch and Go* (Edinburgh: Saint Andrew Press, 2002).

Galloway, Kathy, *Walking in Darkness and Light* (Edinburgh: Saint Andrew Press, 2001).

Guinness, Michele, *Made for Each Other* (London: Triangle, 1996).

Guinness, Michele, *Woman: The Full Story* (Grand Rapids, MI: Zondervan, 2003).

Hammond, Catherine, *Cultivating All-Age Worship* (Warwick: CPAS, 2000).

Harvey, Ruth (ed.), *Wrestling and Resting* (London: CTBI, 1999).

Irvine, Effie, *A Journey of Faith* (Washington, DC: Serendipity, 2003).

John, Killy and Alie Stibbe (eds), *Bursting at the Seams* (Oxford: Monarch Books, 2004).

Levison, Mary, *Wrestling with the Church* (London: Arthur James, 1992).

Macdonald, Lesley Orr (ed.), *In Good Company: Women in Ministry* (Glasgow: Wild Goose Publications, 1999).

Mead, Joy, *A Telling Place* (Glasgow: Wild Goose Publications, 2002).

Morley, Janet (ed.), *All Desires Known* (London: SPCK, 1992).

Pickard, Jan Sutch (ed.), *Dandelions and Thistles* (Glasgow: Wild Goose Publications, 1999).

The St Hilda Community, *Women Included* (London: SPCK, 1991).

Ward, Hannah, Jennifer Wild and Janet Morley (eds), *Celebrating Women* (London: SPCK, 1995).

Yoder, June Alliman, Marlene Kropf and Rebecca Slough, *Preparing Sunday Dinner: A Collaborative Approach to Worship and Preaching* (Scottsdale, PA and Waterloo, Ontario: Herald Press, 2005).

General Index

Index of
Biblical References